Frederic:	*A paradox?*
King:	*A paradox!*
Ruth:	*A most ingenious paradox!* *We've quips and quibbles heard in flocks,* *But none to beat this paradox!...*
Frederic:	*How quaint the ways of paradox!*
Ruth, King:	*A paradox, a paradox,* *A most ingenious paradox.*

—Gilbert & Sullivan, The Pirates of Penzance, Act II

Paradox for Windows

Version 1.0

Getting Started

Borland International, Inc.   1800 Green Hills Road
P.O. Box 660001, Scotts Valley, CA 95067-0001, USA

CONTENTS

EXAMPLES

TABLES

FIGURES

CHAPTER 1

Introduction

Paradox for Windows brings to the Microsoft® Windows environment the fast, full-featured, and easy-to-use relational database package already meeting the information management needs of thousands of users.

Paradox is designed for computer users with all levels of experience, from beginners to advanced. It gives you the power of a full-featured relational database without the need for programming.

What is Paradox?

A paradox is something that appears to be a contradiction but is, in fact, true. For example, powerful database programs have typically been difficult to learn and slow to act. The paradox of Paradox is that this sophisticated database program is powerful and capable of handling complex tasks, yet easy to learn and swift to act.

Paradox is a full-featured relational database management system that you can use either as a standalone system on a single computer or as a multiuser system on a network. If you sometimes feel overwhelmed by the vast quantity or variety of data you work with, Paradox is for you. It lets you control the expanding volumes of data you work with daily.

Perhaps a better question than "What is Paradox?" is "What can Paradox do for me?" The simple answer is that Paradox can manage your data at whatever level you need.

The needs of a database user often grow over time. At first it's important to be able to create a table quickly and easily, enter data in the table, ask questions about the data, and generate a report. These essential tasks never lose their importance, but as your needs expand, the power of your database system must expand with them.

Data has a tendency to grow over time. It's important to be able to break data into small, easily managed tables. It's then important to be able to link tables easily so you can query data across several tables and create multi-table forms and reports. Paradox gives you the power to do this simply and quickly.

You'll also find that the more you work with a system, the more you'll want to customize it. At first, you may just want to enhance a report's visual appeal, or create customized forms for ease of data entry. Later, you may want to perform some tasks automatically or tie several tasks together.

Paradox's rich set of design features can give you the exact look you want for your forms and reports. You can draw from the data in many tables, and add summary and calculated fields to make conclusions about the data. You can include graphs and crosstabs of your data to inform with visual impact. Then you can add ObjectPAL code to objects on forms to create any function you need. You can even create buttons that you click to execute commands you define.

The ultimate power Paradox gives you is the ability to create your own database applications. You can use ObjectPAL to create a whole database application, define its menus, organize and structure the tables it uses, define the functions you want, and deliver the whole application. Once an application has been delivered, any ObjectPAL code is hidden from the user, so the customization of Paradox is transparent. For information on working with ObjectPAL, refer to the *Guide to ObjectPAL*.

What is a relational database?

A database is an organized collection of information or data. An address book is a simple example of a database. It organizes data about people into specific categories: names, phone numbers, and addresses.

In a relational database like Paradox, data is organized into tables. Tables contain categories of data, repeated for each item in the table. For example, if you structure an address book as a table, you might put names in one column, addresses in another, phone numbers in another, and so on. For each person in the address book (each item in the table), you enter the same categories of data (name, address, phone number).

A relational database lets you define a relationship (called a *link*) between different tables. This lets you extract or combine data from several tables and get the exact results you need.

How to use this manual

Getting Started explains how to install Paradox and introduces you to its basic features. Each step-by-step lesson demonstrates a specific task or process. You can read the entire manual as a tutorial or use individual exercises to answer specific questions.

A word about Windows

To gain the full benefits of Paradox, you should first familiarize yourself with Windows. This manual assumes you know how to use Windows and uses Windows-specific terminology. For help with Windows, see your Windows documentation.

Terms and conventions

The Paradox manuals use certain terms and conventions to refer to specific actions and objects. Although many of these conventions may seem intuitive, use this section as a reference if you get stuck.

Mouse terms

These terms indicate specific mouse actions:

□ *Point* means to move the pointer to a specific object. For example, to point to a SpeedBar button, move the mouse until the tip of the pointer touches the button.

In certain functions, the pointer changes shape and indicates you perform an action with the mouse. For example, if the pointer changes to a double-headed arrow, you can drag the object in the directions indicated by the arrow.

□ *Click* means to press the *left* mouse button while pointing to an object. For example, to click the Folder SpeedBar button, point to it on the SpeedBar, then click the left mouse button once.

□ *Double-click* means to rapidly press the *left* mouse button twice while pointing to an object. For example, to choose a specific file from a list, point to the file name, then double-click it.

□ *Drag* means to hold down the *left* mouse button while moving the mouse. Depending on the type of object selected, dragging resizes or moves an object.

□ *Right-click* means to press the *right* mouse button while pointing to an object. For example, to display an object's menu, point to the object, then right-click it.

Keyboard terms

These terms indicate specific keyboard actions:

❑ *Press* means to press a specific key on your keyboard. For example, "press *Enter*" means "press the *Enter* key." (On your keyboard, this key may be labeled with the word *Return* or with the symbol ↵.)

❑ *Type* tells you specific information to type from the keyboard. For example, type **C:\PDOXWIN\SAMPLE** means to type those characters on the keyboard, exactly as given.

❑ *Enter* is a general term referring to information that cannot be expressed with explicit instructions. For example, "Enter the current date" means if today is December 31, 1992, type **12/31/92**.

General terms

These terms indicate specific mouse *or* keyboard actions using standard Windows techniques:

❑ *Choose* means to pick a specific menu command or object using the technique you're most comfortable with. For example, to "choose File | Open" you can use the mouse (by clicking the menu bar to open the File menu, then clicking the Open command) or the keyboard (by pressing *Alt+F*, pressing ↓, then pressing *Enter*).

❑ *Select* means to pick an object. For example, to "select the Customer Number field" while viewing a table means to click it with the mouse or to press the ← or → keys until that field is selected.

❑ *Inspect* means to use the Object Inspector to view or change an object's properties. The easiest way to inspect an object is to right-click it with the mouse. For more information, see Chapter 4.

See also For more information about terms and definitions used in the Paradox manuals, refer to the glossary in the *User's Guide*. Appendix A in the *User's Guide* lists keyboard actions and shortcuts.

Printing conventions

The Paradox manuals use printing conventions to help you distinguish keyboard keys, names of Paradox objects, menu commands, user-entered text, and so on. These conventions exist only to make the manuals more readable—you don't have to observe them when you use Paradox.

Table 1-1 Printing conventions used in this manual

Convention	Applies to	Examples
Bold	Any message displayed by Paradox	Paradox displays the message **Index Error on Key Field**
Italic	Names of Paradox objects, glossary terms, example elements, emphasized words	*Answer* table, *relational database*
ALL CAPS	DOS files and directories, reserved words, operators, types of queries	SAMPLE directory, CUSTOMER.DB, C:\WINDOWS
Initial Caps	Fields, menu commands, object names	Price field, Edit I Cut command, Custord form
Keycap font	Keys on your keyboard	*F1, Enter*
Monospaced font	ObjectPAL code	`myTable.open("sites.db")`
Type-in font	Text that you type in	**CALC Price * Qty**

How to contact Borland

Borland offers a variety of services to answer your questions about Paradox. These services are available in every country where Paradox is sold and vary from country to country. For the most up-to-date information on contacting Borland, see the brochure on registering your product included with Paradox.

Registering your copy of Paradox

To register your copy of Paradox, complete and return your registration card. You can also register by calling 800-845-0147 (within the U.S. and Canada) or by contacting your local Borland representative (elsewhere).

To register your copy
800-845-0147
(U.S. and Canada)

When you register, you immediately become eligible for

❑ Free access to Borland's world-class technical support. (Technical support is free unless the product was purchased under a program that specifies otherwise. You must pay telephone toll charges on technical support calls. Support, upgrade, and product information policies are subject to change. These terms and conditions are for U.S. and Canadian customers only.)

❑ Advance notice of new versions and special prices.

❑ Information on Borland's database development and product enhancements, as well as information on other new Borland products.

Resources in your package

Your Paradox package contains many resources to help you:

❏ The manuals provide information on every aspect of the program. Use them as your main information source.

❏ While using the program, you can press *F1*, use the Help menu, or choose the Help button for help.

❏ Many common questions are answered in the README file located in the system files directory. Additional online information files on specific topics might also be included. The manuals refer to these files where appropriate.

Borland resources

Borland Technical Support publishes technical information sheets on a variety of topics and is available to answer your questions.

TechFax
800-822-4269 (voice)
(U.S. and Canada)

TechFax is a 24-hour automated service (available in the U.S. and Canada) that sends technical information to your fax machine. You can use your touch-tone phone to request up to three documents per call.

File Download BBS
9600 Baud, 8, N, 1

The Borland File Download BBS has sample files, applications, and technical information you can receive by using your modem. No special setup is required.

Country	Modem number
U.S. and Canada	408-439-9096
Australia	(02) 911-1024

Online information services

Worldwide subscribers to the CompuServe, GEnie, or BIX information services can receive technical support by modem. Use the commands in the following table to contact Borland while accessing an information service.

Service	Command
CompuServe	GO BORLAND
BIX	JOIN BORLAND
GEnie	BORLAND

Address electronic messages to *Sysop* or *All*. Don't include your serial number; messages are in public view unless sent by a service's private mail system. Include as much information on the question as possible; the support staff will reply to the message within one working day.

Paradox Technical Support

Paradox Technical Support is available weekdays during business hours to answer any technical questions you have about Paradox.

Country	Phone number
U.S. and Canada	408-461-9166
	6:00 a.m. to 5:00 p.m. Pacific time
U.K.	0734 320777
Australia	(02) 911-1022

Paradox Technical Advisor
900-555-1006 (voice)
(U.S. only)

When you need an instant answer or more advanced technical support (within the U.S.), you can call Borland's Technical Advisor service at 900-555-1006. You gain access within one minute. The first minute is free and there is a charge for each additional minute. The Technical Advisor Line operates weekdays from 6:00 a.m. to 5:00 p.m. Pacific time.

Information you need when
you call Technical Support

When you call Technical Support, call from a telephone near your computer, and have the program running. Keep the following information handy to help process your call:

❏ Product name, serial number, and version number

❏ The brand and model of any hardware in your system

❏ Operating system and version number (use the DOS VER command to find your DOS version number, and choose Help | About Program Manager to find your Windows version number)

❏ Contents of your AUTOEXEC.BAT and CONFIG.SYS files (located in the root directory (\) of your computer's boot disk)

❏ The contents of your WIN.INI and SYSTEM.INI files (located in your Windows directory)

❏ A daytime phone number where you can be contacted

❏ Your network name and software version number, if you're running Paradox on a network

❏ If the call concerns a problem, the steps to reproduce the problem

You can also send support inquiries by fax or the postal system. For addresses and fax numbers, see the brochure on registering your product. Be sure to include the information listed in the preceding section.

Borland Technical Support also publishes technical information sheets on a variety of topics.

Customer Service   Borland Customer Service is available weekdays during business hours to answer any nontechnical questions you have about Borland products, including pricing information, upgrades, and order status.

Country	Phone number
U.S.	408-461-9000
	7:00 a.m. to 5:00 p.m. Pacific time
Canada	416-229-6000
U.K.	0734 321150
Australia	(02) 911-1033

Exploring Paradox

This part of *Getting Started* tells you how to install Paradox and contains a tutorial showing how to use it. Part I contains the following chapters:

❏ Chapter 2, "Installing and starting Paradox," tells you how to install Paradox and explains how to get it running on your copy of Windows or OS/2 2.0.

❏ Chapter 3, "What Paradox can do for you," describes how Paradox can help you manage the information and data you use every day.

❏ Chapter 4, "Becoming familiar with Paradox," defines basic terms and concepts, shows you how to work with Paradox, and how to get help.

❏ Chapter 5, "Working with tables," shows how to view and work with tables in Paradox.

❏ Chapter 6, "Creating new tables," shows how to create a table in Paradox.

❏ Chapter 7, "Using forms and reports," shows how to create, use, and print forms and reports.

❏ Chapter 8, "Designing new forms," shows how to create, display, and save forms.

❏ Chapter 9, "Designing new reports," shows how to create, preview, and save new reports.

❏ Chapter 10, "Designing mailing labels," shows how to create a report to print mailing labels.

❏ Chapter 11, "Querying your data," shows how to use queries to ask questions of your data.

❏ Chapter 12, "Changing tables with queries," shows how to design queries that work with more than one table, including queries that display information from two tables, insert records from one table into another, and change the values of a field to the values in a another table's field.

❏ Chapter 13, "Managing your files," shows how to use folders, aliases, and the File Browser.

CHAPTER 2

Installing and starting Paradox

You should be familiar with Windows before installing Paradox.

This chapter explains

❏ What you need to install and use Paradox

❏ How to install Paradox

❏ How to start and exit Paradox

After finishing this chapter, you'll be ready to learn how to use Paradox to manage your data.

Before you start

Before installing Paradox,

❏ Check the contents of your Paradox package

❏ Make sure you have the correct equipment and operating system for running Paradox

❏ Make a backup of the Paradox disks

What's included with Paradox

Before installing Paradox, make sure you have the following items in your package:

❏ *Getting Started*

❏ *User's Guide*

❏ *Quick Reference*

❏ *Guide to ObjectPAL*

❏ Paradox software disks and function-key template

System requirements

Paradox requires the hardware and software described in Table 2-1.

Table 2-1 System requirements for installing and running Paradox

Component	Description/Comments
Microprocessor	80386 or higher.
RAM	4MB. Performance will increase with more memory.
Hard disk	A hard disk is required. You need at least 20MB of free disk space to install Paradox and use it effectively. The Paradox system files take 15MB.
Video monitor	EGA or higher. CGA video cards are not supported.
Microsoft Windows	Version 3.1 or later, Version 3.0 is not supported.
Mouse	Although not required, a mouse is *strongly* recommended. Some design features can be accessed only with a mouse.
Network	A network is not required, but Paradox supports the following networks: Novell Advanced Netware, 3COM 3Plus/3Plus Open, Microsoft LAN Manager, and any network that is 100% Windows compatible.

Making a backup copy

Before you install Paradox, make a complete backup copy of the program disks. Use your backup copy to install the program, and store your original disks in a secure place. You might need to reinstall or recopy the sample files.

To make a backup copy of the Paradox disks, use the MS-DOS DISKCOPY command or the Windows Program Manager. For more information, consult your MS-DOS reference manual or your Windows documentation.

Installing Paradox

Before you install Paradox, you need the following information:

❑ Your name and the name of your company.

❑ The serial number printed on the label of Paradox Disk 1.

❑ The drive (or directory) you're installing Paradox from. Usually, this will be either A or B.

❑ The directory where you want the Paradox system files located. By default, INSTALL stores these files in C:\PDOXWIN.

❑ The directory where you want to store the ODAPI files. ODAPI (for Object Database Architecture Programming Interface) lets Paradox share tables and other files directly with other Borland

Windows products, such as the Database Desktop provided with Quattro Pro for Windows.

Important   If you have other Borland products that use ODAPI, install Paradox's ODAPI files in the same directory you installed the other product's ODAPI files.

By default, INSTALL places these files in your WINDOWS\ SYSTEM directory.

❏   The directory where you want to store the sample files (optional). By default, these are placed in C:\PDOXWIN\SAMPLE. You'll need the sample files to use the tutorial in Chapters 4 through 13 of this manual.

❏   The directory where you want to store the ObjectPAL examples (optional). By default, INSTALL places these files in C:\PDOXWIN\EXAMPLES.

❏   The directory where you want to store the ObjectPAL Dive Planner sample application (optional). By default, INSTALL places these files in C:\PDOXWIN\DIVEPLAN.

Note   If you're installing and using Paradox on a network drive or in an international (non-U.S.) setting, see Chapters 15 and 16 before installing Paradox. These chapters contain important information about using Paradox in these situations.

What INSTALL does

When you run INSTALL, it does the following:

❏   Creates the directories you specify (if necessary)

❏   Verifies your serial number

❏   Modifies your WIN.INI file so Paradox runs properly in Windows

❏   Copies the Paradox system files, the ODAPI files, and (optionally) the sample files to your hard disk

❏   Creates a Paradox for Windows group for your Paradox icons in Program Manager (optional)

❏   Copies icons into Program Manager for Paradox and its utilities

❏   Configures ODAPI to use the data formats for the country defined in Windows Control Panel

If you install Paradox on a local (non-network) drive, INSTALL creates two directories below the system directory:

❏   WORKING is the default working directory.

❏   PRIVATE is the directory used for temporary files.

See also   For more information about working directories, see Chapter 4. For information about private directories, see Chapter 15 in this manual and Chapters 2 and 3 in the *User's Guide*.

Starting INSTALL

To start the Paradox INSTALL program in Windows, follow the steps outlined here. If your Windows directory is on the DOS PATH, you can start Windows and INSTALL from the DOS prompt by typing **a:\install**, provided Windows is *not* already running.

1. Start Windows.

If you want to install from drive B, change all references to A in these instructions to B.

2. Put Paradox Program Disk 1 in drive A.

3. Choose File I Run from the Program Manager main menu.

4. In the Command Line text box, type **a:\install**, then choose OK. This opens the Paradox for Windows Installation dialog box.

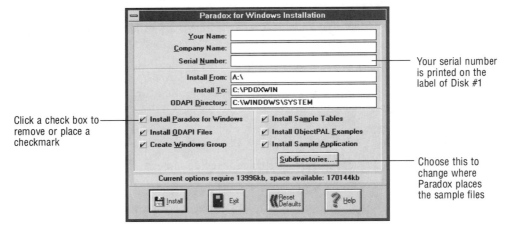

Your serial number is printed on the label of Disk #1

Click a check box to remove or place a checkmark

Choose this to change where Paradox places the sample files

5. Enter the necessary information. Use the mouse (or press *Tab* and *Shift+Tab*) to select different text boxes.

6. Choose Install to install the files you selected.

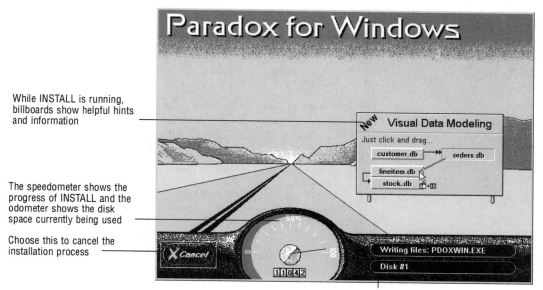

While INSTALL is running, billboards show helpful hints and information

The speedometer shows the progress of INSTALL and the odometer shows the disk space currently being used

Choose this to cancel the installation process

These panels tell you what file and disk INSTALL is currently working with

Note Periodically, Paradox displays a New Disk dialog box, as shown in Figure 2-1. When this happens, insert the appropriate disk in drive A, then choose OK.

Figure 2-1 The New Disk dialog box

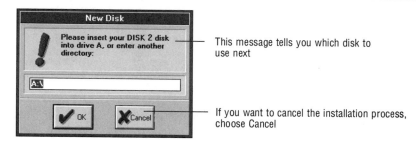

This message tells you which disk to use next

If you want to cancel the installation process, choose Cancel

The README file contains important, late-breaking information.

When the Paradox system files are completely installed, INSTALL displays the README file.

If you chose to create a Windows group for Paradox from the Paradox for Windows Installation dialog box, INSTALL creates a Paradox for Windows group, then places the Paradox icons in it. Otherwise, the Paradox icons are copied into the active Windows group.

Installing specific files

If you decide to install any of the files later, you can start INSTALL again, and check only the options you want to install.

Installing SHARE

To ensure the integrity of your data, load the DOS SHARE utility before starting Windows. You *must* install SHARE if you plan to

❐ Run Paradox while other applications are using Paradox files. These applications could be ObjectVision, dBASE, Quattro Pro, Sidekick, and applications developed with the Paradox Engine.

❐ Use multiple instances of Paradox (or other ODAPI-hosted applications) to access the same tables on your local drive.

❐ Run Paradox under certain network configurations. To determine if SHARE is required for your network, contact your network administrator.

To see if SHARE is already loaded on your computer, exit Windows, type **share** at the DOS prompt, then press *Enter*. If SHARE is already loaded, you'll see the message **SHARE already loaded**; otherwise, this command loads SHARE.

Note   Running DOS from *within* Windows always reports that SHARE is loaded, even when it isn't. Test for SHARE *before* you start Windows. If you've already loaded Windows, exit before testing for SHARE.

To install SHARE automatically,

❐ If you have an AUTOEXEC.BAT file, type **c:\dos\share** before the WIN command that starts Windows.

❐ If you don't have an AUTOEXEC.BAT file, create an ASCII text file, type **c:\dos\share**, then save it as C:\AUTOEXEC.BAT. When finished, restart your workstation.

Note   If your DOS system files are not stored in C:\DOS, change these references to the appropriate path.

Adjusting CONFIG.SYS and AUTOEXEC.BAT

Before starting Paradox, you need to verify a few settings in your CONFIG.SYS and AUTOEXEC.BAT files:

❐ Your CONFIG.SYS file should set FILES to at least 60 and BUFFERS to at least 40.

❐ If you install ODAPI to a directory other than WINDOWS\SYSTEM, add that directory to the PATH= statement in your AUTOEXEC.BAT file. The DOS PATH *must* include this directory; otherwise, you will not be able to start Paradox.

❐ If you want to use DDE or OLE with Paradox, add your Paradox system directory to your DOS PATH.

If you modify your CONFIG.SYS or AUTOEXEC.BAT files, be sure to exit Windows and restart your workstation so your changes take effect.

Tip   If you use SMARTDRV.EXE (or another disk cache), you can reduce the BUFFERS setting in CONFIG.SYS to 10.

See also   For information about changing CONFIG.SYS and AUTOEXEC.BAT, consult your Windows documentation.

Reading the README file

If Paradox has changed since the manuals were printed, the changes are described in the README file. This file also contains late-breaking news and tips. To display or print this file, use Notepad, any text editor, or a word processor.

Icons placed in Program Manager

After Paradox is installed, several icons appear in the Program Manager. The Paradox icon lets you start Paradox, and the other icons start utility programs. The following list describes each icon and shows where to find more information:

 The Paradox for Windows icon starts Paradox. For more information, see "Starting Paradox" later in this chapter.

 The Configuration Utility lets you configure ODAPI. For more information, see Chapter 14.

 The Serial Number Utility lets you add user counts to Paradox. For more information, see Chapter 15.

 The Local Settings Utility lets you change the directories used by Paradox. For more information, see Chapter 15.

 The Table Utility lets you test and repair (if necessary) damaged tables and indexes. For more information, see the README.TXT file.

Notes for OS/2

You can install and use Paradox under versions of OS/2 that fully support Windows 3.1. Use WIN-OS/2 full-screen mode and install Paradox the same way you install any other Windows 3.1 application.

After installing Paradox, add the ODAPI directory to your LIBPATH= statement in CONFIG.SYS. Other configuration settings may be necessary, depending on your version of OS/2.

See also   For more information, see your OS/2 documentation.

Starting Paradox for Windows

You can start Paradox in two ways:

☐ Double-click the Paradox for Windows icon.

☐ Use the mouse or the keyboard to select the Paradox icon, then choose File I Open from the Program Manager main menu.

Tip If your Windows directory is on the DOS PATH, you can start Windows and Paradox from the DOS prompt by typing **pdoxwin**, provided Windows is *not* already running. This starts Windows, then starts Paradox.

Note Some of Paradox's files are used by other Borland applications, such as Borland C++ or Quattro Pro for Windows. If you have these files and Paradox uses revised versions, the files are updated the first time you start Paradox.

When Paradox is loaded, the Desktop appears, as shown in Figure 2-2.

Figure 2-2 The Paradox Desktop at startup

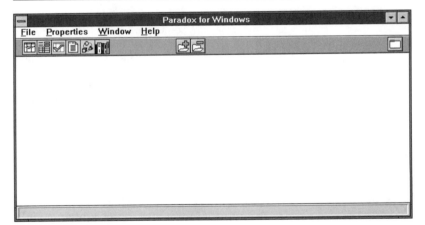

See also Chapter 4 describes the Desktop and how to use it.

Exiting Paradox

You can exit Paradox in several ways:

❐ Double-click the Desktop Control menu.

❐ Choose Close from the Desktop Control menu.

❐ Choose File | Exit.

❐ Press *Alt+F4*.

If you exit Paradox after changing any files and you haven't saved your changes, Paradox asks if you want to save the changes. Choose Yes to save your changes or No to discard them.

When you exit Paradox, you return to the Windows Program Manager.

CHAPTER 3

What Paradox can do for you

Whether you're new to database programs or have used other products, this chapter shows how Paradox can fill your data management needs. It offers hints and suggestions by describing the development of a business application.

Important   This chapter is not a tutorial. Instead, it provides an overview of Paradox and ideas for different ways to accomplish your tasks. It describes concepts and features not otherwise discussed in this manual (such as key fields, secondary indexes, and referential integrity). For information about these concepts, consult the *User's Guide*.

You can find a tutorial in Chapters 4 through 13 of this manual.

The MAST company

If you haven't installed the sample files, refer to "Installing Paradox" in Chapter 2.

Throughout the Paradox manuals, you'll see examples using the sample files included with Paradox. These files manage information for the fictitious Marine Adventures & Sunken Treasures (MAST) company. MAST sells diving equipment and arranges diving expeditions. Like most companies, MAST tracks information about customers, orders, inventory stock, and vendors. Because they arrange diving expeditions, they also deal with dive sites, shipwrecks, and marine life.

MAST's customers are dive shops around the world. They sell supplies to and arrange trips for these shops. The shops place orders for equipment and make reservations for groups of divers.

This section describes how MAST grew as a company and how Paradox filled MAST's information management needs at each stage of development.

Stage one: A single table

William Budd founded MAST knowing information is an important commodity, like the diving masks and air regulators he would sell. He needed a powerful database program for his personal computer, but didn't want to invest a lot of time and money in learning a complex product. So, he bought Paradox, and found all the power he needed in an intuitive, easy-to-learn Windows application.

In Paradox, information (or data) is stored in tables.

The first table Will created was all he thought he needed. He listed all the information he wanted to track, and created a table with a structure that looked like this:

Field name	Field type	Field size	Explanation
Customer	A	30	Name of dive shop
Address	A	50	Customer's address
Phone	A	15	Customer's phone number
Item	A	50	Item ordered
Qty	N		Quantity ordered
Price	$		Price of item
Date	D		Date of order
Delivery	D		Promised delivery date
Terms	A	6	Terms of payment
Part No	A	15	Vendor's part number
List Price	$		Vendor's price
Vendor	A	30	Vendor's company name
V Address	A	50	Vendor's address
V Phone	A	15	Vendor's phone number

Each field holds one piece of information.

Will understood that different types of data should be defined as different field types, and he kept field sizes to a minimum to conserve disk space.

When a customer placed an order, Will filled in the fields of the table, took the item from stock, shipped it, and ordered a replacement from the vendor. It all seemed to work pretty well.

Queries let you ask questions of your data.

At the end of each month, Will performed a query on the table, and got an *Answer* table listing the orders placed during the month. He then created a report based on *Answer* to bill each customer.

But it soon became apparent that there were some problems with this system.

Stage two: The need for a primary key

Will started getting phone calls from angry customers. A dive shop in Florida had received three separate bills for the three items they had placed on the same order. Another shop got a bill late because it had been sent to the wrong address. A customer in Hawaii got billed twice for the same order.

Primary keys sort your tables and help prevent duplicate data.

Will began to get regular complaints, and he realized it was due to inefficient information management. So, he created a primary key for the table.

A composite key is a primary key made up of more than one field.

A primary key ensures that each record of the table is unique, so customers could never be billed twice for the same item. Since no one field of his table was unique, Will created a *composite* key. A composite key combines the values in two or more fields for the key's identification.

Will decided that no two records should ever have the same combination of Customer, Item, and Date values. The combination of these values (the composite key) would have to be unique for each record. This made sense. How many times would a customer ever place more than one order for the same thing on the same day?

Group bands let you create reports that group related records together.

Will also created a smarter report. He created a *group band* that grouped the records according to Customer. Using this design, even if a customer placed more than one order during the month, they received only one bill, listing each item.

So two of the problems with MAST's information management system were solved—a customer would never receive two bills for the same order, nor individual bills for individual items on the same order. To solve the problem of an incorrect address, Will needed a way to make sure the values he entered were accurate every time.

Stage three: Organizing smaller tables

Will realized that each time he entered information in the table, he risked making a mistake. He was entering the same information over and over again. A customer who placed 20 orders had been entered in the table 20 times. That meant 20 chances for error in the customer's name, address, or phone number. After reading the *User's Guide*, he realized he could work with his data more easily and increase its integrity if he divided the original table into several smaller ones. When necessary, he could link them together.

This time Will did some planning before he structured his tables. As he planned his tables, he realized that

❒ Each table should contain an obvious field to use as a primary key.

❒ To link tables, he'd need to duplicate some fields (and data) between his tables, but he should duplicate only the fields (and data) needed to link the tables.

Secondary indexes establish an alternate sort order for a table.

❒ A table must have a primary key or a secondary index assigned to the matching field before it can be linked to another table.

Referential integrity makes sure changes made to one table are reflected in another.

❏ Fields that *are* duplicated between tables should use referential integrity to make sure their values match in all tables.

When finished, Will created six tables to manage the data of his original table. These tables comprise the sample files included with Paradox.

See also   For a full description of key fields, secondary indexes, and referential integrity, see Chapters 2 and 9 in the *User's Guide*.

The Customer table

When planning the *Customer* table, Will split the information about a customer's address into separate fields. This let him perform queries about specific states or countries. He realized he could use queries to combine these fields together, if necessary. Will learned that it's easier to work with small pieces of information separately than with large pieces of information. The *Customer* table looked like this:

Field name	Type	Size	Linking	Explanation
Customer No	N		P*	Unique customer number
Name	A	30		Name of dive shop
Street	A	30		Street address
City	A	15		Customer's city
State/Prov	A	20		State or province
Zip/Postal Code	A	10		Zip code or postal route
Country	A	20		Customer's country
Phone	A	15		Customer's phone number
First Contact	D			Date of first contact with customer

* P = Primary key

The Orders table

When he created the *Orders* table, Will knew he would need to link it to the *Customer* table. He had to associate an order with a customer somehow. So, he placed the primary key from *Customer* (Customer No) in *Orders*, then defined a secondary index for it. This meant the two tables could be sorted (and linked) in the same order.

When he did this, Will realized that the value he entered as a Customer No in *Orders* had to be valid and match a record in *Customer*; otherwise, the new *Orders* record was meaningless. So, he established referential integrity between the Customer No field in both tables.

Will also wanted to keep his order information separate from the item(s) being ordered. So, he included only information about the order itself in the *Orders* table. It looked like this:

Field name	Type	Size	Linking	Explanation
Order No	N		P*	Unique order number
Customer No	N		S, R	Secondary index and referential integrity to Customer No in *Customer*
Sale Date	D			Date of order
Ship Date	D			Date to be shipped
Ship VIA	A	7		Cargo carrier used
Total Invoice	$			Cost of total order
Amount Paid	$			Amount paid so far
Balance Due	$			Due after partial payment
Terms	A	6		Terms of payment
Payment Method	A	7		Cash, charge, etc.
Month	A	3		Month order was placed

* P = Primary key, S = Secondary index, R = Referential integrity

The Lineitem table

Will wanted his customers to be able to order as many items at a time as they wanted. To do this, he created a separate table, called *Lineitem*, for the items being ordered.

The primary key of *Lineitem* is a composite of the Order No and Stock No fields; these fields also have secondary indexes. This lets *Lineitem* link to *Orders* (using Order No) and *Stock* (using Stock No). To protect the integrity of the *Lineitem* information, Will defined referential integrity to the tables he planned to link to, using the same fields. *Lineitem* looked like this:

Field name	Type	Size	Linking	Explanation
Order No	N		C, S, R*	The combination of Order No and Stock No
Stock No	N		C, S, R	The unique value for each item stocked
Selling Price	$			Price charged to customer
Qty	N			Number of items ordered
Total	$			Total of Selling Price * Qty

* C = Composite key, S = Secondary index, R = Referential integrity

The Stock table

Will also wanted a clear understanding of his stock on hand, so he could order products more efficiently. To do this, he created *Stock* so it could be linked to *Lineitem* and *Vendors*.

Stock No is the primary key for this table. Because Stock No is a secondary index in *Lineitem*, the two tables can be linked. Vendor No is the primary key of *Vendors*, so it had to be a secondary index in

Stock, and needed referential integrity to check against values in Vendor No in *Vendors.* The *Stock* table looked like this:

Field name	Type	Size	Linking	Explanation
Stock No	N		P*	Unique stock number
Vendor No	N		S, R	Secondary index and referential integrity to Vendor No in *Vendors*
Equipment Class	A	30		Category of stock
Model	A	20		Vendor's model name
Part No	A	15		Vendor's part number
Description	A	30		Quick description of item
Catalog Description	F	10		Full catalog description of item
Qty	N			Quantity in stock
List Price	$			Vendor's list price

* P = Primary key, S = Secondary index, R = Referential integrity

The Vendors table

Next, Will created a table for his vendors. Here, as in *Customer,* he remembered to divide addresses across fields. *Vendors* looked like this:

Field name	Type	Size	Linking	Explanation
Vendor No	N		P*	Unique vendor ID number
Vendor Name	A	30		Company name
Street	A	30		Street address
City	A	20		Vendor's city
State/Prov	A	20		State or province
Country	A	15		Vendor's country
Zip/Postal Rt	A	10		Zip code or postal route
Phone	A	15		Phone number
FAX	A	15		FAX number
Preferred	A	3		Indicate preferred status

* P = Primary key

Using this system, he knew that a customer's information was entered only once, and then referred to by other tables. Likewise, order, item, stock, and vendor information was entered only once. The chance for errors was substantially reduced.

When all the tables were created, Will used INSERT queries to move his existing data into the new structures. He knew he would probably never have to link *all* the tables, only a few at a time, but he wanted to see what his company's data model looked like with all the changes he had made. He quickly linked the tables, and saw the data model shown in Figure 3-1.

Figure 3-1 MAST system data model

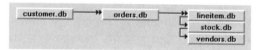

Finally, Will needed a way to keep track of who to reach at each customer site. So, he created *Contacts* and filled it with the name and telephone number of the person he talked to the most often at each site. *Contacts* looked like this:

Field name	Type	Size	Linking	Explanation
Last Name	A	10		Contact's last name
First Name	A	20		Contact's first name
Company	A	30		Contact's company name
Phone	A	15		Contact's direct phone

With *Contacts*, Will was able to keep track of information that didn't need to fit into his data model. He kept its information separate and was able to protect the privacy of his contacts and their direct phone numbers.

Stage four: Creating multi-table documents

MAST was really taking off, and Paradox supported its growing information needs. Will needed some powerful data entry forms and reports to maximize the power of his data model.

A data entry form

To enter new orders, Will created a form linking *Customer, Orders*, and *Lineitem*. Paradox used the keys and secondary indexes to figure out how to link the tables. The form Will created is shown in Figure 3-2.

Figure 3-2 A multi-table data entry form

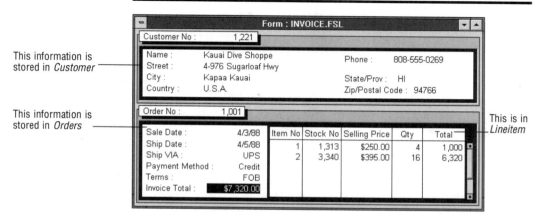

Will let Paradox do more work for him by calculating the value of Total Invoice in *Orders* from the Selling Price and Qty fields of *Lineitem*. He inspected the Total Invoice field, defined it as a calculated field, and set up the calculation **Lineitem.Selling Price * Lineitem.Qty**. From then on, Paradox totaled the invoice for him.

A multi-table report

Besides being able to enter orders more efficiently, Will found he could communicate more effectively with his customers. For example, he created a multi-table report to show his customers their buying practices. The report linked *Customer* to *Orders* and presented information from both tables in a standard letter format, as shown in Figure 3-3.

Figure 3-3 A multi-table report

To our friends at Cayman Divers World Unlimited:

I'm pleased to be able to offer this summary of the orders you've placed with MAST and hope it helps you gain an insight to your company's buying practices.

I'd like to help you take advantage of quantity discounts and automatic delivery schedules. We have a number of programs available and I'm sure one would fit your needs perfectly. Please feel free to call me at our toll-free number; I'll be happy to make the best arrangements.

Your orders are shown in the following table:

Order No	Sale Date	Ship Date	Ship VIA	Total Invoice	Terms	Pymt Method
1,004	4/17/88	4/28/88	DHL	$3,525.00	FOB	Check
1,104	7/17/89	7/24/89	DHL	$51,673.15	FOB	Check
1,192	8/30/90	9/8/90	FedEx	$1,305.10	Net 30	Visa
1,292	5/30/91	5/31/91	FedEx	$7,986.90	Net 30	Visa
1,392	1/30/92	2/3/92	FedEx	$16,102.00	Net 30	Visa

I hope this information is as valuable as your business is to MAST.

Stage five: Creating and saving queries

As MAST grew and evolved, Will needed to know more about the information in his tables. He found he was constantly using queries to ask questions about his data. For example,

❑ When he considered opening a new branch, he asked questions like how many customers do we have in each state? Which state generates the most revenue for us? Where are our vendors most centrally located? Is there a correlation between vendor location and customer location?

❑ When Will considered changing his domestic long-distance service, he asked questions like how many customers do we have in this state? How many in this time zone? How many in this country? What percentage of our phone calls are international?

❑ Each month Will performed the same queries, to see how sales compared to the previous month, the previous quarter, and the previous year. He could then calculate forecasts for the coming months. He learned early that he could save a query and reuse it month after month.

Stage six: Creating a report from a query

Will had always run a query and then created a report based on the *Answer* table to print his results. One day, he noticed he could create a report based on a saved query. This was interesting. He opened a new report, chose Queries from Type drop-down list of the Data Model dialog box, chose the query he ran each month, designed the report, and then saved it. Each time Will printed his new report, Paradox automatically ran the query and printed the results. Will found he could print the latest information almost effortlessly; Paradox was now doing even more work for him.

Stage seven: Organizing working directories

Eventually, Will decided to expand MAST's business to include the organization of diving expeditions. He knew information management would be crucial to this side of the business, and that his business would now exist in two very distinct parts. He wanted a way to organize all the files he was currently using and to keep them separate from the new ones he would create. He found that Paradox had provided a means to do that all along.

Will never paid much attention to working directories because he really didn't need to. Now, with his business growing, he had two distinct businesses. He knew how to organize files into subdirectories at the DOS level, so he created a directory called DIVEPLAN and used this to store the files for that side of his business. Then, he created *aliases* for his directories so he could change his working directory easily and quickly.

Aliases are directory shortcuts.

Stage eight: Building the Dive Planner in ObjectPAL

Will's work went smoothly. Pretty soon, his customers began asking to browse through the expeditions he offered without him standing over their shoulders. After Will read about ObjectPAL and worked through the examples in *Guide to ObjectPAL*, he created an application for his customers.

Will created a number of forms containing buttons, then attached *methods* to them, which displayed other forms and automatically updated his Dive Planner tables. This let him control what happened behind the scenes. When his customers used the Dive Planner, they found the standard Windows controls they were used to, such as pop-up help, dialog boxes, menus, and many others.

After testing his application with a few customers, Will decided it was finished, *delivered* the forms (to protect their designs), and created a *script* to start the Dive Planner. All a customer had to do was open the script and start using the buttons and other controls. Will set up the Dive Planner on a separate workstation and sent copies of it to his other offices.

Understanding relationships

Much of Will's success was possible because he defined relationships between (or linked) his tables. By doing so, he was able to minimize the amount of

❑ Work he had to do to maintain the information in his tables

❑ Time it took for Paradox to perform his tasks

❑ Disk space used by his tables

Ideally, a table contains data about one specific type of thing. For example, records in the *Orders* table contain only the information specific to an individual order, such as the order number, the date it was placed, the invoice total, and so on. The only information about the customer who placed the order is an ID number that refers to a record in another table called *Customer*.

In the sample tables, the records in *Orders* describe one type of thing (orders) while the records in *Customer* describe another (customers). Using different tables to keep track of different types of information offers many advantages. For example, you can

❑ Save time when entering information because you don't have to retype a customer's name, address, and phone number when they place another order.

❑ Save disk space because you won't have several records containing the same information.

❑ Make fewer mistakes. If you spelled a customer's name right the first time, it's spelled correctly on all subsequent orders.

❑ Save maintenance time. If the customer moves, you need to change only one record, not several.

To gain these benefits, create forms and reports that link your tables. For example, Figure 3-4 shows a form linking the *Orders* and *Customer* tables.

Figure 3-4 The *Orders* and *Customer* tables

These tables can be linked because they contain the same information in the Customer No fields

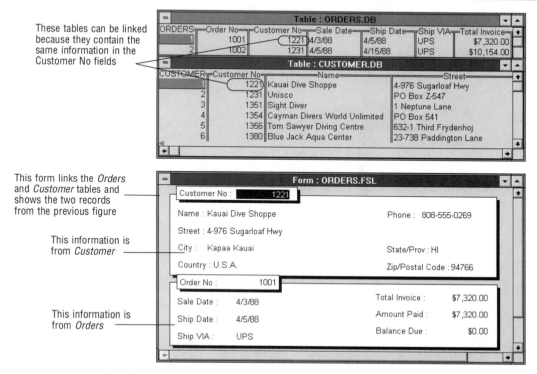

This form links the *Orders* and *Customer* tables and shows the two records from the previous figure

This information is from *Customer*

This information is from *Orders*

See also See Chapter 10 of the *User's Guide* for more information on linking tables.

Not the end of the story

As his business flourished, Will's work with Paradox continued. At every step of the way, there was another feature in Paradox that made his information easier to manage.

At this point, you have an idea of how useful Paradox can be for your data management.

From here, begin working through the tutorial, which starts in Chapter 4. As you become more experienced with Paradox, refer to Will's story from time to time. Every so often, you'll find something that makes your data easier to manage.

Becoming familiar with Paradox

This chapter explains what you need to learn Paradox. It describes

❐ Basic terms and concepts

❐ What you already know about using Paradox

❐ The Paradox Desktop

❐ The working directory and how to change it

❐ How to use online help

Data basics

As you work with Paradox, you'll encounter a number of new terms and concepts. This section explains many of these.

See also For help with any Paradox term or concept, see the Help system (described later in this chapter) or the glossary in the *User's Guide*.

Database

A *database* is an organized collection of related information (or data) stored for easy, efficient use. An address book is a database, as is the card catalog in a library, a company's general ledger, and a completed tax form. In Paradox, a database is a collection of one or more tables used to keep track of information.

Tables

A *table* is where you store your data. Tables are organized into horizontal rows (records) and vertical columns (fields). This makes it easy to examine or change your data. Figure 4-1 shows the sample *Orders* table.

Figure 4-1 The *Orders* table

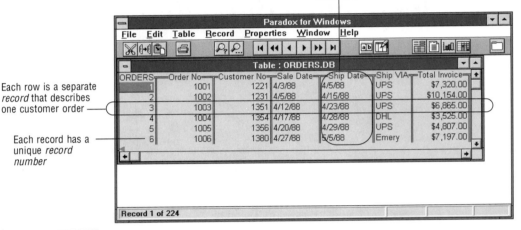

Each column is a *field* that contains one
category of information about a customer

Each row is a separate
record that describes
one customer order

Each record has a
unique *record
number*

Records

A horizontal row (or *record*) in a table contains information about an individual person, place, or thing, depending on what the table tracks. In the *Orders* table, each record describes an order placed with the MAST company; it tells you who placed the order, when it was placed, when it was shipped, and so on. Thus, each row in the *Orders* table is made up of several categories of information about one specific thing—a customer's order.

Fields

A vertical column in a table is a *field*. Each field contains one category of information about the person, place, or thing described in the record. In the *Orders* table, Order No is one field, Customer No another, and so on.

Information in a specific field is called a *field value*.

Record number

The *record number* is an internal counter Paradox uses to keep track of each record. Paradox manages record numbers automatically, so you cannot change them directly.

Field types

The *field type* tells Paradox what sort of information a specific field can hold and what actions can be performed with that field's data. Some common field types include: alphanumeric (or character), number, date, currency, and memo. Paradox tables also support *blob* (binary large objects) *fields*, which hold specialized information, such as formatted memos, graphic images, and OLE links.

See also

Paradox also lets you create and use tables from other applications, such as dBASE, DOS Paradox, ObjectVision, Sidekick 2.0, and many others. For a full discussion of the table types and field types supported by Paradox, see Chapter 2 in the *User's Guide*.

Files

Paradox saves your work in files. For a complete list of file types and extensions, see Chapter 2 in the *User's Guide*.

Design documents

Design documents let you present your data in new or different ways. Paradox supports two types of design documents:

☐ *Forms* let you edit and display data in various ways, including combining data from more than one table. You can also create forms to do some of your work for you.

☐ *Reports* print your table data. Like forms, they let you define relationships between tables. Unlike forms, they do not let you edit your tables.

In Paradox, each type of design document shares some of the characteristics of the other. Each document type has strengths and advantages; use the type appropriate for your needs.

Objects

In everyday life, nearly everything you encounter is an object. This manual is an object, your Paradox disks are objects, and so on. Likewise, almost everything in Paradox is an object. An object can be a table, form, field, window or file.

Once you learn to work with one type of object, you can work with similar objects. For example, when you know how to edit tables using Table windows, you can also edit tables using Form windows. When you know how to design forms, you have the basics of designing reports.

Properties

Properties are characteristics and behaviors of objects, such as color, shape, position, or text style. You can change the appearance or behavior of an object by changing its properties. Each object has unique properties.

The Object Inspector

Paradox's Object Inspector™ feature lets you view, or *inspect*, an object's menu, which contains properties for the object. To inspect an object, you right-click it. You can use the object's menu to change the object's appearance or behavior.

See also

For more information, see Chapter 2 in the *User's Guide*.

Relationships   Paradox is a relational database; this means you can establish *relationships*, or links, between two tables.

What you already know about using Paradox

Since Paradox is a Windows application, you probably already know a great deal about using it. For example,

❐ To open a menu, click it with the mouse, or hold the *Alt* key and then press the underlined letter on the menu bar. (To open the File menu, press *Alt+F*.)

❐ To move a window, point to the window's title bar, press and hold the left mouse button, then drag the window to where you want it. To move a window using the keyboard, use the window's Control menu.

❐ To resize a window, move the pointer so it touches a border of the window, press and hold the left mouse button, then drag the border to where you want it.

❐ To tile, cascade, or close all open windows, use the Window menu.

❐ To close any window in Paradox, double-click its Control menu or press *Ctrl+F4*.

❐ To select different options in dialog boxes, click an option with the mouse or use *Tab* and *Shift+Tab*.

❐ Use the Cut and Paste SpeedBar buttons (or *Shift+Del* and *Shift+Ins*) to cut and paste information to the Windows Clipboard.

❐ To quickly open Paradox's Control menu, click the upper left corner of the Desktop window or press *Alt+Space*. To quickly open the Control menu of a window on the Desktop, click its upper left corner or press *Alt+Hyphen*.

In general, if you don't know how to do something in Paradox, but you know how to do it in Windows, try the same method. It will probably work.

The Paradox Desktop

When you start Paradox, the Desktop appears, as shown in Figure 4-2.

Figure 4-2 The Paradox Desktop at startup

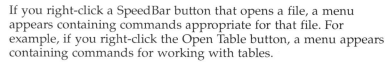

Control menu
Menu bar
SpeedBar
Title bar
Minimize button
Maximize button
Window border
Status bar

The Desktop is the central working area in Paradox. You start all tasks from the Desktop.

The Desktop contains a number of areas you should be familiar with:

❒ The *menu bar* contains commands you can choose to open windows, configure your Desktop, and work with your data.

The menu bar contains only the menus you need at the moment. If a menu isn't appropriate for a given task, it doesn't appear on the menu bar.

❒ The *SpeedBar* contains shortcut buttons for common menu commands. Like the menu bar, the SpeedBar buttons change as you open different windows.

To choose a SpeedBar button, click it with the mouse. To see what function a SpeedBar button performs, simply point to it. A description of its function appears in the status bar.

If you right-click a SpeedBar button that opens a file, a menu appears containing commands appropriate for that file. For example, if you right-click the Open Table button, a menu appears containing commands for working with tables.

❒ The *status bar* gives you information about the task you're working on and the current state of Paradox. Like the menu bar and the SpeedBar, the appearance of the status bar changes as you work.

❒ Standard Windows controls, like the title bar, the borders, the Control menu, the Maximize button, and the Minimize button, let you control the shape, size, and position of the Desktop.

See also Chapter 3 of the *User's Guide* describes the Desktop in more detail.

The working directory

A Paradox *working directory* contains the tables and files you're currently working with. A working directory lets you indicate where you want Paradox to look for your files and controls the files that are listed in the File | Open and File | Save dialog boxes.

Changing the working directory

When you save a new file, Paradox places it in the working directory, unless you include a directory path with the object's name. To use files in a different directory, choose File | Working Directory to change to that directory before creating or opening the file.

If you installed Paradox on a local (non-network) drive, your default working directory is set to a directory called WORKING. This directory is created by INSTALL and placed below your Paradox system directory. For example, if you used the default directories when installing Paradox, your default is C:\PDOXWIN\WORKING.

Tip Because Paradox is a large application, it's a good idea to place your files (tables, forms, reports, and so on) in a different directory than your Paradox system directory. This gives you the best performance and makes it easier to back up your data.

Note When you change the working directory, Paradox closes any open windows on the Desktop before changing to the new directory.

Changing to the SAMPLE directory

Paradox's sample files are located in the SAMPLE directory. If you did not install the sample files when you installed Paradox, install them now. (See Chapter 2 for information about installing the sample files.) Unless otherwise indicated, the examples in this manual refer to files in the SAMPLE directory.

Note If you're running Paradox from a network, contact your network administrator for the location of the sample files.

Example 4-1 Changing to the SAMPLE directory

To use the sample files provided with Paradox, change to the directory where these files are located:

1. From the Desktop, choose File | Working Directory. The Set Working Directory dialog box appears.

The OK button is dimmed until you enter an existing directory that Paradox can find. When the OK button is dimmed, you cannot choose it.

2. If you installed the sample files in the default directory, type **c:\pdoxwin\sample**. If you installed the sample files in a different directory, type that directory's name instead.

3. Choose OK.

This manual introduces you to the basic skills you need to use Paradox; you can sharpen these skills by experimenting with the sample files. The more time you spend working with tables and design documents, the easier it will be for you to use Paradox.

Note   Paradox often offers many ways to accomplish a given task. Don't feel limited by the techniques discussed in this manual. If you prefer a different approach for a particular task, use it instead. This manual often uses the quickest way to perform a task.

Tip   For best performance, use working directories extensively. If you have more than 80 files in a directory, you should create and use a new working directory.

Using online Help

If you get stuck while using Paradox, use the online Help system by choosing Help | Contents, pressing *F1*, or choosing a Help button from a dialog box.

Example 4-2 Getting help with Paradox

Suppose you want general help with Paradox's basic concepts and skills.

1. From the Desktop, choose Help | Contents. The Help Contents screen appears.

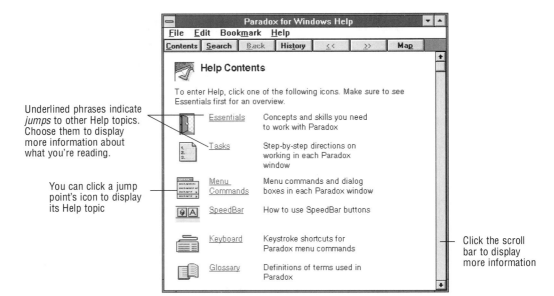

Underlined phrases indicate *jumps* to other Help topics. Choose them to display more information about what you're reading.

You can click a jump point's icon to display its Help topic

Click the scroll bar to display more information

2. Choose Essentials. You'll see a list of topics containing basic information about using Paradox, as shown in the following figure:

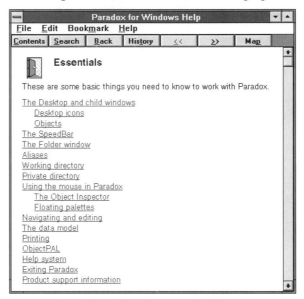

Buttons in the Paradox Help window

The Paradox Help window contains buttons to help you find the information you want.

Contents ❑ Contents returns you to the Contents screen of the current Help file.

Search ❑ Search lets you locate a specific Help topic by browsing an index of terms and concepts.

Back ❑ Back returns you to Help topics you've displayed during the current Help session.

History ❑ History lists the topics you've displayed in the current Help session. Use this to return quickly to a specific topic.

<< ❑ Browse Backward (<<) steps you backward through a list of related Help topics, whether or not you've viewed them in the current Help session.

>> ❑ Browse Forward (>>) steps you through a list of related Help topics.

Home ❑ Home takes you to the Help|Contents topic.

Map ❑ Map displays a chart of the Help system. You can click an area to view its topics.

 To close the Paradox Help windows, double-click the Control menu or press *Alt+F4*.

See also For more information about Paradox's Help system, choose Help system from the list of Essentials topics.

Locating specific Help topics

The Map and Search buttons let you find specific Paradox Help topics.

Using the Help map

The Map button presents a chart to the Paradox Help system. To display a topic, click it with the mouse.

Example 4-3 Using the Help map

Suppose you want to use the Help map to display the Essentials topic.

Contents 1. Make sure you've opened the Help Window and are viewing the Help Contents topic. (If this topic isn't displayed, choose the Contents button.)

Map 2. Choose the Map button. The Paradox Help map appears.

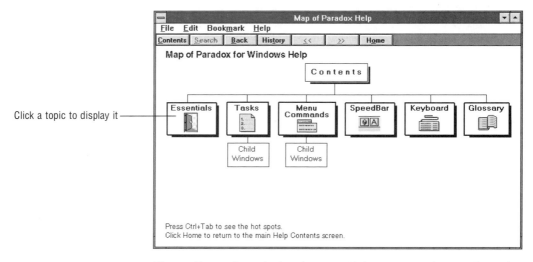

Click a topic to display it ——

3. Choose Essentials to display the same Help topic you chose in Example 4-2.

Tip When using the Help files, press and hold *Ctrl+Tab* to see *hot zones* to other Help topics. To choose a hot zone, click it with the mouse.

Searching for specific Help topics

The Search button lets you find selected topics in the Help files.

Example 4-4 Searching for a specific Help topic

Suppose you want to find more information about the Paradox Desktop.

Contents
1. Make sure you've opened the Help window and are viewing the Help Contents topic. (If this topic isn't displayed, choose the Contents button.)

Search
2. Choose the Search button. The Search dialog box appears, as shown in the following figure:

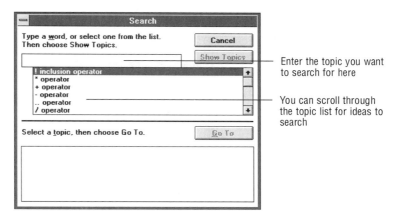

Enter the topic you want to search for here

You can scroll through the topic list for ideas to search

3. Type **desktop**. As you type, the topic list adjusts, displaying topics beginning with the letters you type.

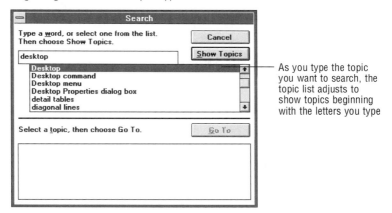

As you type the topic you want to search, the topic list adjusts to show topics beginning with the letters you type

4. Choose Show Topics. A list of Help topics appears.

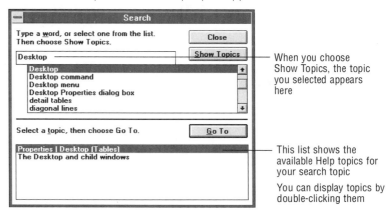

When you choose Show Topics, the topic you selected appears here

This list shows the available Help topics for your search topic

You can display topics by double-clicking them

5. Choose the topic titled "The Desktop and child windows," then choose Go To. The first Help topic about the Desktop appears, as shown in the following figure:

Tips for using Help

❏ Place *bookmarks* in Help files to locate topics you refer to often.

❏ Use *annotations* to add your own remarks and comments to the Paradox Help files.

❏ Keep the Help window open when you're working on unfamiliar features in Paradox. Open the Help window, resize it, and move it to a corner of the screen, so you can switch to it quickly.

See also For more information about bookmarks and annotations, see your Windows documentation or choose Help I Using Help.

CHAPTER 5

Working with tables

Tables are the objects you'll use the most in Paradox. This chapter shows you how to

❑ Access the sample tables

❑ Open and use a Table window

❑ Replace, change, and locate field values

❑ Add and delete records

Note   The examples in this chapter refer to the sample tables provided with Paradox. If you did not install the sample files when you installed Paradox, do so now. For help, see Chapter 2.

What is a table?

In Paradox, information is stored in *tables*. Tables are lists of information arranged in meaningful ways. For example, you can use a table to keep track of customer lists, inventory records, employee rosters, comments about sales contacts, parts lists, and so on.

Figure 5-1 shows a Table window and how to change its appearance with the mouse.

Figure 5-1   A Table window showing the *Customer* table

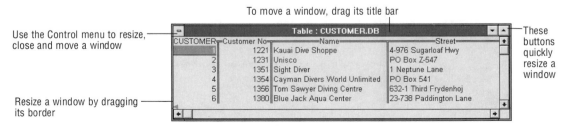

To move a window, drag its title bar

Use the Control menu to resize, close and move a window

These buttons quickly resize a window

Resize a window by dragging its border

CUSTOMER	Customer No	Name	Street
1	1221	Kauai Dive Shoppe	4-976 Sugarloaf Hwy
2	1231	Unisco	PO Box Z-547
3	1351	Sight Diver	1 Neptune Lane
4	1354	Cayman Divers World Unlimited	PO Box 541
5	1356	Tom Sawyer Diving Centre	632-1 Third Frydenhoj
6	1380	Blue Jack Aqua Center	23-738 Paddington Lane

Table : CUSTOMER.DB

Viewing a table

To display (or *view*) the data in a table, click the Open Table SpeedBar button or choose File I Open I Table.

Example 5-1   Opening a table

To view the *Customer* table,

1. Make sure you're working in the SAMPLE directory. (For help, see Chapter 4.)

2. Click the Open Table SpeedBar button. The Open Table dialog box appears, which lists all the tables in the working directory.

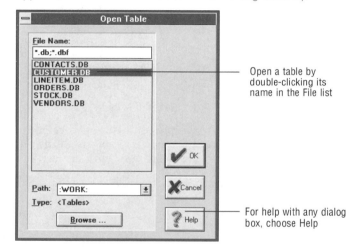

Open a table by double-clicking its name in the File list

For help with any dialog box, choose Help

3. Choose CUSTOMER.DB, then choose OK. Paradox opens a Table window containing the *Customer* table.

To close a window, double-click its Control menu

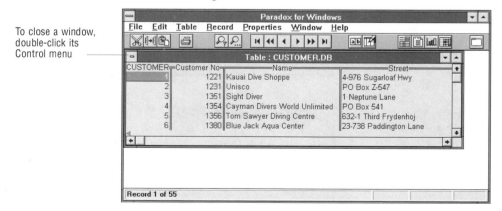

To display as much of the table as possible, maximize the Desktop and Table windows by clicking both Maximize buttons or by choosing Maximize from both Control menus.

Changing table properties

Tables have properties that you can set to change the way Paradox displays your data. Figure 5-2 shows some of the changes you can make.

Figure 5-2 Table properties you can set

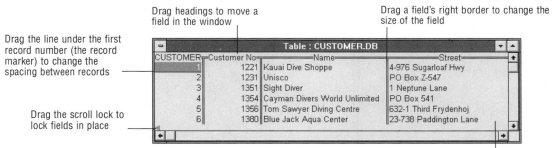

Drag headings to move a field in the window

Drag a field's right border to change the size of the field

Drag the line under the first record number (the record marker) to change the spacing between records

Drag the scroll lock to lock fields in place

Inspect fields to change formats, fonts, and colors

You can change the properties of the Table window and its contents by using the mouse and the Object Inspector.

Example 5-2 Changing the properties of a table

Suppose you want to place lines between the records in the table you viewed in Example 5-1.

1. Make sure you're viewing the *Customer* table. (If you need help, see Example 5-1.)

2. Point to the vertical line between the record number and the Customer No fields of record 1.

Inspect the grid to change its colors or to display lines between records

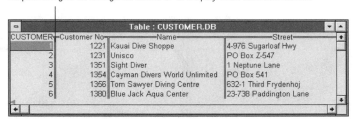

3. When the pointer becomes a double-headed arrow, inspect the grid by clicking the *right* mouse button once. The grid's menu appears.

4. Choose Grid Lines⏐Row Lines. Paradox now displays lines between each record in the *Customer* table.

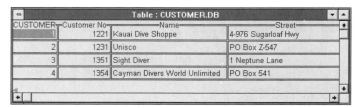

5. Experiment with the mouse and the Object Inspector by changing a number of different properties. When the pointer changes to different shapes, see what you can do with the mouse. Also, point to other areas of the table, then inspect them to see other properties you can change.

Restoring property settings

You can restore a table's properties with Properties ⏐ View Properties ⏐ Restore. This resets the window's properties to the last saved settings.

Example 5-3 Restoring property settings

Suppose you want the *Customer* table displayed as it was when you viewed it in Example 5-1.

1. Choose Properties⏐View Properties⏐Restore. Paradox restores the table to its earlier appearance.

To save property changes, choose Properties ⏐ View Properties ⏐ Save.

See also For more information about table properties, see Chapter 4 in the *User's Guide*.

Selecting records and fields

When working with tables, you'll want to select different records and fields. Figure 5-3 shows how to do this with the mouse.

Figure 5-3 Selecting fields and records with the mouse

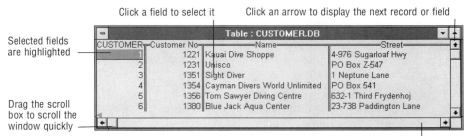

Click a field to select it   Click an arrow to display the next record or field

Selected fields are highlighted

Drag the scroll box to scroll the window quickly

Click a scroll bar to display the next set of records or fields

You can also use the Record menu, the keyboard, or the SpeedBar to select different fields and records.

Using the Record menu

The Record menu lets you select different records. These commands are most useful for casual browsing.

Example 5-4 Selecting records with the Record menu

To select different records with the Record menu,

1. Make sure you're viewing the *Customer* table. (See Example 5-1 if you need help.)

2. When you open a table, the first record number is selected. Choose Record|Next to select the second record number.

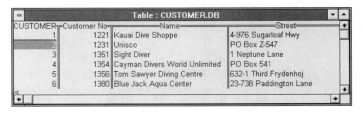

3. Choose Record|Next Set to select the next set of records in the table. The Table window scrolls and displays the next set of records.

A set of records is the number of records that fit in a window

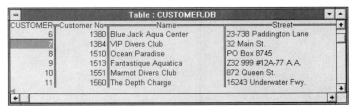

4. Choose Record|Previous to select the previous record.

5. Experiment with other Record commands to become familiar with their actions.

Shortcut   You can choose many menu commands with keyboard shortcuts. For example, pressing *Shift+F12* is the shortcut for Record I Next Set. When a menu command has a shortcut, the key is described next to the command on the menu. Try repeating Example 5-4 using shortcut keys.

See also   For a full list of keys and what they do, see Appendix A in the *User's Guide*.

Using the keyboard

When you enter new records or change existing ones, the keyboard is useful for selecting different fields quickly. Table 5-1 shows what several keys do in a Table window.

Table 5-1 Keys to use in Table windows

Key	Effect/Action
←	Selects the field to the left of the selected field
→	Selects the field to the right of the selected field
↓	Selects the same field in the record below the current one
↑	Selects the same field in the record above the current one
Home	Selects the first field in the current record
End	Selects the last field in the current record
Ctrl+Home	Selects the first field of the first record in the table
Ctrl+End	Selects the last field of the last record in the table
PgDn	Displays the next set of records
PgUp	Displays the previous set of records
Ctrl+PgDn	Scrolls the window to the next set of fields
Ctrl+PgUp	Scrolls the window to the previous set of fields

The following example demonstrates some of these keys.

Example 5-5 Using the keyboard to select different fields

To select different fields with the keyboard,

1. Make sure you're viewing the *Customer* table. (See Example 5-1 if you need help.)

2. Press *Ctrl+Home* to select the record number of the first record.

3. Press → to select the Customer No field.

4. Press ↓ to select the Customer No field for record 2.

5. Press *End* to select the last field (First Contact) of record 2.

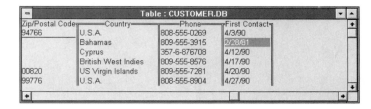

The First Contact field is selected

6. Experiment with different keys to get a feel for each one.

Note   If you experience trouble using the keypad keys, make sure Num Lock is off.

Using the SpeedBar

When a Table window is active, the SpeedBar contains shortcut buttons for commands on the Record menu.

Example 5-6 Moving through a table with the SpeedBar

To select different fields and records using the SpeedBar,

1. Make sure you're viewing the *Customer* table.

2. Click the First Record SpeedBar button. This displays the first record in the table.

3. Click the Next Record SpeedBar button. This selects the same field in the second record in the table.

4. Experiment with other SpeedBar buttons.

See also   For more information about moving through a table, see Chapter 4 of the *User's Guide*.

Editing tables

When you want to add new records or change data in existing ones, enter Edit mode while viewing the table.

Example 5-7 Entering Edit mode

To enter Edit mode,

1. Make sure you're viewing the *Customer* table.

2. Click the Edit Data SpeedBar button to enter Edit mode. Paradox indicates the mode change in the status bar.

The Edit Data SpeedBar button appears pressed in edit mode

			Paradox for Windows					▼ ▲
File	Edit	Table	Record	Properties	Window	Help		

⊟	Table : CUSTOMER.DB		▼ ▲

CUSTOMER	Customer No	Name	Street	
1	1221	Kauai Dive Shoppe	4-976 Sugarloaf Hwy	
2	1231	Unisco	PO Box Z-547	
3	1351	Sight Diver	1 Neptune Lane	
4	1354	Cayman Divers World Unlimited	PO Box 541	
5	1356	Tom Sawyer Diving Centre	632-1 Third Frydenhoj	
6	1380	Blue Jack Aqua Center	23-738 Paddington Lane	

Record 1 of 55		Edit	

Status bar indicates Edit mode

3. Click the Edit Data SpeedBar button to exit Edit mode.

Shortcut You can also enter Edit mode by clicking the Edit Data SpeedBar button, choosing Table I Edit Data, or pressing *F9*.

Replacing a field value

To change a field's *entire* value, select the field, then begin typing. Paradox replaces the old value with the one you type.

Example 5-8 Replacing a field value

Suppose one of your customers, Kauai Dive Shoppe, gets a new phone number. To update your *Customer* table accordingly,

1. Make sure you're viewing the *Customer* table.

2. Click the Edit Data SpeedBar button to enter Edit mode.

3. Select the Phone field for Kauai Dive Shoppe, the first record in the table. (See Example 5-4 through Example 5-6.)

4. Enter your phone number into the field, then exit Edit mode to save your change.

Paradox saves your changes when you either exit Edit mode, select a different record, or insert a new record.

See also For more information about Edit mode, see Chapter 5 in the *User's Guide*.

Changing a field value

To change only part of a field's value, use Field View.

Example 5-9 Changing part of a field's value

Suppose you want to change the area code of the phone number you changed in Example 5-8.

1. Make sure you're viewing the *Customer* table.

2. Enter Edit mode. (If you need help, see Example 5-7.)

3. Select the Phone field for Kauai Dive Shoppe.

4. Click the Field View SpeedBar button to enter Field View. Paradox indicates the mode change in the status bar and places an insertion point in the field.

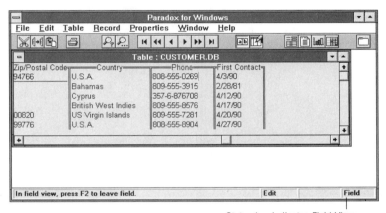

Status bar indicates Field View

When you enter Field View, some keys on the numeric keypad act differently. For more information, see the User's Guide.

5. Press **Home** to move the insertion point to the beginning of the field.

6. Press **Del** three times to delete the current area code.

7. Type **555**.

Insertion point follows the text as you type

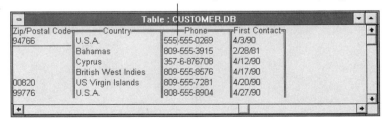

8. Click the Field View SpeedBar button to exit Field View. When you exit Field View, the insertion point disappears, the message in the status bar goes away, and the field you changed is selected. Notice that you are still in Edit mode.

9. Exit Edit mode to save your change.

Shortcut You can also enter Field View by selecting a field and then clicking it with the mouse. When you do this, the insertion point appears at the place you click. For example, if you clicked the left side of the Phone field (after selecting it) in the previous example, steps 4 and 5 would have happened at the same time.

See also For a full description of Field View, see Chapter 5 of the *User's Guide*.

Adding records

To add a new record to a table,

1. Open the table in a Table window.

2. Enter Edit mode.

3. Insert a blank record by choosing Record | Insert, pressing *Ins* or moving past the last record in the table.

4. Use the keyboard to fill in the empty fields.

The following example walks you through each of these steps.

Example 5-10 Adding a record to a table

Suppose you want to add your name and address to the end of the *Customer* table.

1. Make sure you're viewing the table.

2. Enter Edit mode.

3. Click the Last Record SpeedBar button to move to the end of the table.

4. Press ↓ to insert a blank record at the end of the table.

5. In the Customer No field, type **9999**.

6. Select the Name field and fill in the rest of the record with your name, address, telephone number, and today's date.

7. Exit Edit mode to save your new record. In the status bar, Paradox displays the message **Record has been posted**.

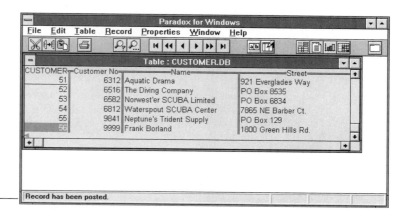

This message indicates the
new record has been saved ——

Tip In Edit mode, Paradox adds blank records when you move past the last record of the table. This is useful when you're adding several records at once; instead of choosing Record | Insert for each record, move to the end of the table, then press ↓ and fill in each blank record as needed.

Note When you add records to keyed tables, Paradox moves the new records to their proper position when they are saved. For example, if you skipped step 3 in Example 5-10, your new record would have jumped to the end of the table when you exited Edit mode.

See also For more information about adding records and keyed tables, see Chapters 5 and 9 in the *User's Guide*.

Deleting records

To delete a record from a table,

1. Open the table in a Table window.

2. Enter Edit mode.

3. Select a field of the record you want to delete.

4. Choose Record | Delete or press *Ctrl+Del*.

Paradox then *permanently* removes that record from the table.

The following example walks you through each of these steps.

Example 5-11 Deleting a record

Suppose you want to delete the record you added in Example 5-10.

1. Make sure you're viewing the *Customer* table.

2. Enter Edit mode.

3. Click the Last Record SpeedBar button.

4. Choose Record | Delete.

5. Exit Edit mode to save your change.

Caution Use care when deleting records, for once a record is deleted, you cannot get it back. (dBASE tables are the *only* exception to this rule.) For more information, see Chapter 4 of the *User's Guide*.

Locating fields and records

When you're working with a large table, locating specific fields, records, or values can be difficult. Use Record | Locate to

❑ Locate a specific field in the current record

❑ Locate a specific record in the table

❑ Locate a record containing a specific field value

❑ Change the same field value in several records

Locating specific fields

You can select a field in the current record with Record | Locate | Field.

Example 5-12 Locating a specific field

Suppose you want to locate the Phone field.

1. Make sure you're viewing the *Customer* table.

2. Click the First Record SpeedBar button (or press **Ctrl+Home**) to select the record number field for Kauai Dive Shoppe.

3. Choose Record | Locate | Field to display the Locate Field dialog box.

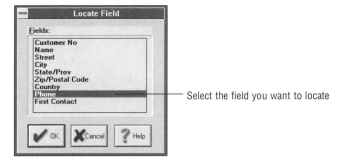

Select the field you want to locate

4. Choose Phone, then choose OK. The Phone field is selected.

The Phone field for Kauai Dive Shoppe

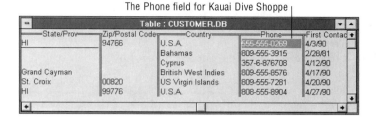

Locating by field values

You can also locate records by their values.

Example 5-13 Locating a field value

Suppose you want to locate a customer in Santa Monica, California.

1. Make sure you're viewing the *Customer* table.

2. Click the Locate Field Value SpeedBar button to display the Locate Value dialog box.

The options in this panel can help locate values. For more information, see Chapter 4 in the *User's Guide*.

Type your search value here

Choose the field you want to search

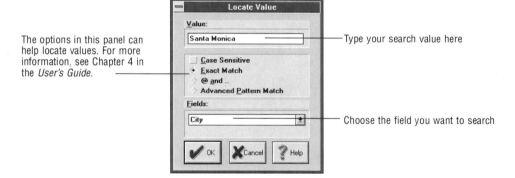

3. Type **Santa Monica.**

4. Under Fields, choose City, then choose OK. Paradox selects the City field for Blue Glass Happiness. The Locate Value dialog box locates the first record containing your value (Santa Monica, in this case) in the field you selected (City).

Blue Glass Happiness is the first customer located in Santa Monica

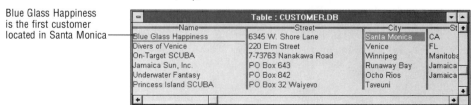

Tip You can also display the Locate Value dialog box by pressing *Ctrl+Z* or by choosing Record I Locate I Value.

Locating by record number

You can locate records by their record numbers.

Example 5-14 Locating a specific record number

Suppose you're viewing *Customer* and want to locate record number 42.

1. Choose Record I Locate I Record Number to display the Locate Record Number dialog box.

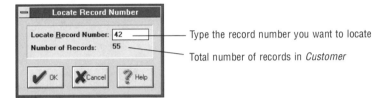

Type the record number you want to locate

Total number of records in *Customer*

2. Type **42**, then choose OK. Paradox locates and displays the record describing Princess Island SCUBA.

Record 42 describes Princess Island SCUBA

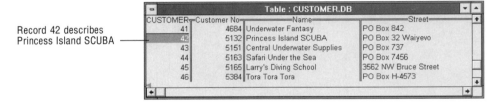

Tips for locating records

The following options make locating records easier and more powerful:

☐ Use Record I Locate Next to repeat a locate operation. When you choose this command, Paradox tries to find another record using the same conditions you entered in the Locate Value dialog box.

☐ When in Edit mode, use Record I Locate and Replace to replace the values of several fields in one operation. For example, you can change all records containing "CA" in the State/Prov field to "California."

See also For more information about locating records, see Chapter 4 of the *User's Guide*.

CHAPTER 6

Creating new tables

This chapter explains how to create a table. It tells you how to

❏ Define and save a table's structure

❏ Display and change a table's structure

To learn these tasks, you'll create a Paradox table called *Address* that you can use later to keep track of addresses.

Creating new tables

To create a table, define its *structure*. Figure 6-1 shows the structure of the *Customer* table you worked with in Chapter 5.

Figure 6-1 The structure of the *Customer* table

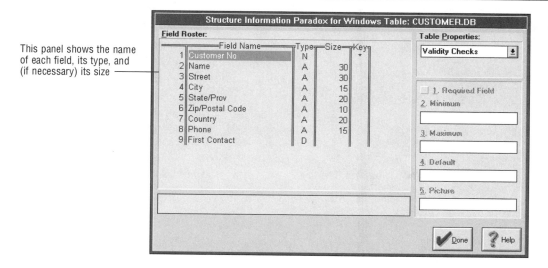

This panel shows the name of each field, its type, and (if necessary) its size

The structure of a table describes the fields in the table and contains the following information:

❐ The name of each field

❐ The type of data each field contains

❐ The size of certain field types, such as alphanumeric or memo fields

❐ The order in which the fields are presented

Planning a table

Before creating a new table, you should plan it:

❐ Pick a name for the table that is easy to remember and is eight characters (or less) in length.

❐ Determine the structure of the table. You should know the name of each field, its type, and its size (if necessary). For a list of field types supported by Paradox, see Chapter 2 in the *User's Guide*.

❐ Decide the order of the fields in the new table.

A table plan can be as simple or as complex as you care to make it; it's a tool to help you define the structure of the table. Figure 6-2 shows a sample plan for the table you'll create in this chapter.

After planning your table, define and save its structure. This is discussed in the next section.

Figure 6-2 A plan for an address table

Field number	Field name	Type	Size
1	Last Name	Alphanumeric	20
2	First Name	Alphanumeric	15
3	Honorific	Alphanumeric	10
4	Company Name	Alphanumeric	30
5	Street	Alphanumeric	30
6	City	Alphanumeric	15
7	State/Prov	Alphanumeric	20
8	Zip/Postal Code	Alphanumeric	10
9	Country	Alphanumeric	15

See also Chapter 9 in the *User's Guide* offers more guidelines for planning tables.

Creating a new table

Creating new tables requires three steps:

1. Choose the type of table you want to create.

2. Describe the fields in the table.

3. Save and name the table.

Choosing a table type

To create a table, begin by right-clicking the Open Table SpeedBar button and choosing New.

Example 6-1 Opening a new table

To create the *Address* table described in Figure 6-2, begin by choosing the Paradox for Windows table type. To do so,

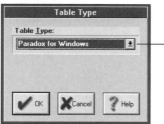

You can also display this dialog box by choosing File|New|Table

1. Right-click the Open Table SpeedBar button, then choose New to display the Table Type dialog box. Paradox for Windows appears in the Table Type panel.

You can create different types of tables. Click the drop-down arrow for a list of available table types

2. Choose OK. This displays the Create Table dialog box.

The title bar shows the table type you're creating

As you work with the Create Table dialog box, this panel displays helpful information

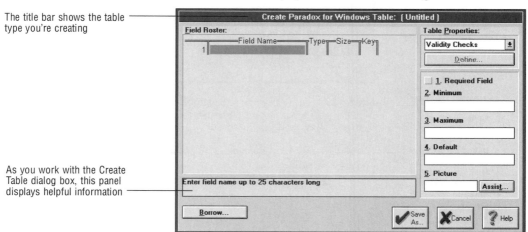

You're now ready to begin defining your new table, *Address*. This is covered in the next example.

Paradox lets you create different types of tables, including Paradox 3.5, dBASE III Plus, and dBASE IV tables.

See also   Chapter 9 in the *User's Guide* contains more information about table types and creating tables.

Defining a new table structure

To define a new table structure, enter the field descriptions into the Field Roster of the Create Table dialog box.

Example 6-2 Defining the fields of a table

Suppose you want to define the table structure shown in Figure 6-2.

1. Make sure you're viewing the Create Table dialog box. (If you need help, see Example 6-1.)

2. In the first Field Name column, type **Last Name**. Press *Tab* to select the Type column.

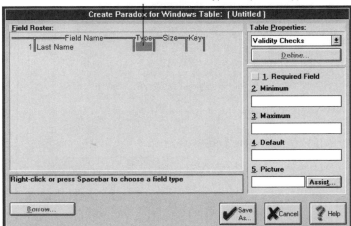

3. Inspect (right-click) the Type column (or press *Spacebar*) to display a menu with the field types you can choose for Paradox tables. Choose Alphanumeric, then press *Tab*.

4. Since alphanumeric field types require a size, type **20**. Press ↓ to add a second row to the Field Roster.

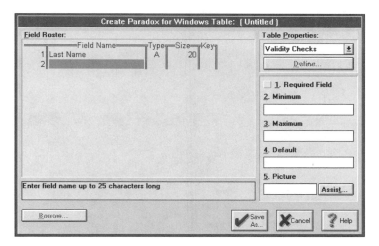

5. Repeat steps 2 through 4 for the rest of the fields described in Figure 6-2. When you finish, your Field Roster should look like the following figure:

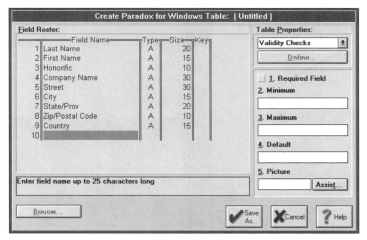

If you made any mistakes, correct them now; otherwise, continue to the next example for information on saving the *Address* table.

Entering information into the Field Roster is like adding records to a table. Use the techniques discussed in Chapter 5 to insert rows, replace values, and correct mistakes in the Field Roster.

Saving a new table structure

Once you've entered a table's structure in the Field Roster, save it to create the table.

Example 6-3 Saving the structure of a new table

If you've worked through the last two examples, you're ready to save the *Address* table. To do so,

1. Make sure you've completed Example 6-1 and Example 6-2.

2. Choose Save As to display the Save Table As dialog box.

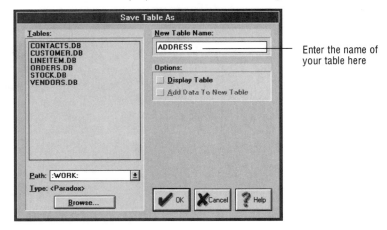

Enter the name of your table here

3. Type **address**.

4. In the Options panel, choose Display Table, then choose OK. Paradox creates, saves, and opens the new table.

Since *Address* was just created, it doesn't contain any records

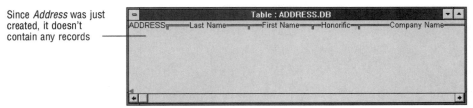

5. You can now edit *Address* and add a few records. If you need help with this, see Chapter 5.

Note   New table structures are created or written to disk only when you save them.

Caution   When choosing a name for a table, do *not* pick a reserved name Paradox gives to temporary tables; otherwise, your table (and data) may be unexpectedly overwritten. For a list of temporary table names, see Chapter 2 in the *User's Guide*.

Displaying and changing a table's structure

To display the structure of a table, open it in a Table window, then choose Table | Info Structure.

Example 6-4 Viewing the structure of an existing table

Suppose you want to view the structure of the *Address* table.

1. Make sure *Address* is open in a Table window. (See Chapter 5 if you need help.)

2. Choose Table | Info Structure to display the Structure Information dialog box, which describes the fields of the *Address* table.

The table type appears in the title bar

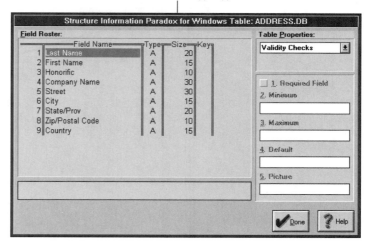

3. To close the Structure Information dialog box, choose Done or press *Esc*.

Tip   You can cancel most Paradox dialog boxes by pressing *Esc*.

Changing the structure of a table

To change the structure of a table, open it in a Table window, then choose Table | Restructure.

Example 6-5 Deleting a field from a table

Suppose you want to delete the Honorific field from your *Address* table.

1. Make sure *Address* is open in a Table window. (If you need help, see Chapter 5.)

2. Choose Table | Restructure to display the Restructure Table dialog box.

Displaying and changing a table's structure

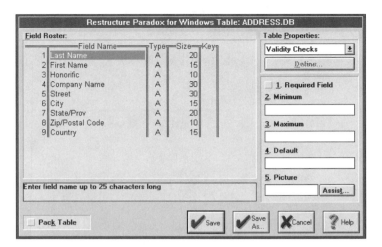

3. Press ↓ two times to select the Honorific field, then press *Ctrl+Del* to delete it.

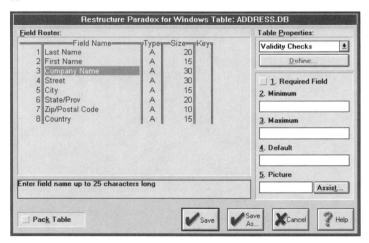

4. Choose Save to save your change. Because you made a change that can remove data from the table, the Restructure Warning dialog box appears.

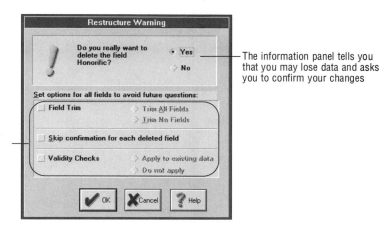

The options in this panel tell Paradox how to handle data that doesn't fit into the new structure. For more information see Chapter 9 in the *User's Guide*.

The information panel tells you that you may lose data and asks you to confirm your changes

5. Choose Yes, then choose OK. Paradox removes Honorific (and any data it contains) from the table and returns to the Table window.

Honorific field is gone

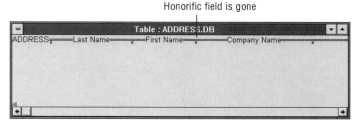

6. Close the Table window.

Caution   Use care when deleting or reducing the size of fields. If you make a change that forces Paradox to remove data from the table, that data is *permanently* removed from the table. It's good practice to make a backup copy of a table *before* restructuring it.

Tip   You can also display and change the structure of a table with the File | Utilities menu. For more information, see Chapter 4 of the *User's Guide*.

See also   Chapter 9 in the *User's Guide* describes the Restructure Warning dialog box and the options it contains.

Tips for creating and restructuring tables

Paradox offers a number of ways to help create new tables and protect the information in your tables. For example, you can

❑ Borrow the structure of existing tables to help create new tables. This saves time and typing. For more information, see Chapter 9 in the *User's Guide*.

❑ Use the *Pack table* check box to remove deleted records from tables.

❑ Format, limit, and protect the data in your tables with the *Table Properties* panel. For example,

❑ Validity checks let you define formats, default values, and data ranges for specific fields.

❑ Table Lookup lets you limit the values of a table to the values contained in another table.

❑ Password Security helps you prevent unauthorized access to your tables.

See also For more information about these and other table features, see Chapter 9 in the *User's Guide*.

CHAPTER 7

Using forms and reports

This chapter shows you how to work with forms and reports. It explains how to

❐ Open, use, and save a quick form

❐ Define a new quick form

❐ Print forms and reports

❐ Print selected pages of a report

❐ Delete a design document

What are forms and reports?

In Paradox, forms and reports are design documents that can present your data in a variety of formats. For example, you can create design documents that

❐ Display one record at a time

❐ Display multiple records at a time

❐ Display only certain fields of a table

❐ Contain design features, such as lines, boxes, graphic images, shading, or special colors

❐ Perform onscreen calculations

Design documents can also link tables together, so information stored in separate tables appears to come from the same place.

The primary difference between the two document types is

❐ Forms are editing tools. They let you display and edit the data in your tables. For example, you can create forms that add data to several tables at once.

❏ Reports are printing tools. They let you format and print your data. For example, you can use reports to create form letters, mailing labels, invoices, presentations, and so on. Reports cannot change the data in your tables, though they can change the way your data appears on the final report.

Figure 7-1 shows a typical form.

Figure 7-1 A form displaying a record in the *Customer* table

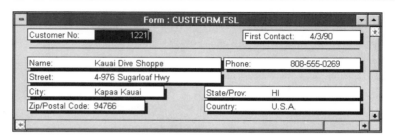

Creating and using a quick form

Before you can use a form, you must create one. You can either create a new form or let Paradox create a quick form after you've opened a Table window.

Creating a quick form

The fastest way to create a form is to open a *quick form* after opening a table in a Table window. By default, quick forms display one record at a time and show each field in the table in a labeled, vertical list.

To open a quick form, open the Table window, then do one of the following:

❏ Click the Quick Form SpeedBar button.

❏ Choose Table | Quick Form.

❏ Press *F7*.

Example 7-1 Creating and opening a quick form

Suppose you want to create a quick form for the *Customer* table.

1. Make sure your working directory is set to the directory containing the sample tables. (If you need help, see Chapter 4.)

2. Use the Open Table SpeedBar button to open the *Customer* table. (If you need help, see Chapter 5.)

3. Click the Quick Form SpeedBar button. Paradox opens a second window containing your form.

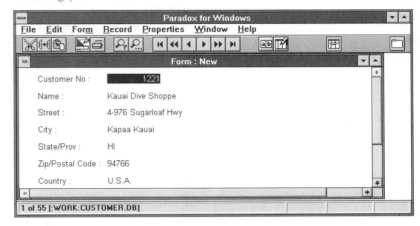

Editing tables in the Form window

When you want to display different records or edit a table's data using a form, use the same techniques you learned in Chapter 5. Specifically, use

❑ Edit mode to change the data in your tables.

❑ The mouse, the SpeedBar, the Record menu, and the keyboard to select and display different fields and records

❑ Field View to edit field values

❑ Record | Insert (*Ins*) and Record | Delete (*Ctrl+Del*) to add and delete records

❑ Record | Locate to locate specific records or values

See also For more information about using forms to work with tables, see Chapters 4 and 5 in the *User's Guide*.

Saving and closing a form

Use File | Save to keep a new form for later use. You can also save a form when you close it.

Example 7-2 Closing and saving a quick form

To close and save the quick form you created in Example 7-1,

1. Make sure you're viewing the form you created in Example 7-1.

2. Click the Design Tool SpeedBar button (or press *F8*) to open the form in a Design window.

3. Choose File | Save to display the Save As dialog box.

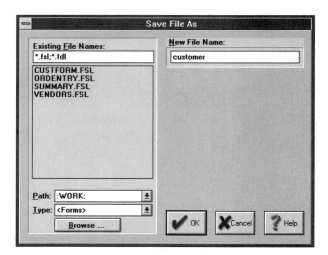

4. Under New File Name, type **customer**, then choose OK. Paradox saves the form to a file called CUSTOMER.FSL.

5. Close the Table and the Form windows by double-clicking their Control menus.

Opening an existing form

To open an existing form, click the Open Form SpeedBar button from the Desktop or choose File | Open | Form.

Example 7-3 Opening and using an existing form

To open the form you saved in Example 7-2,

1. From the Desktop, click the Open Form SpeedBar button to display the Open Document dialog box.

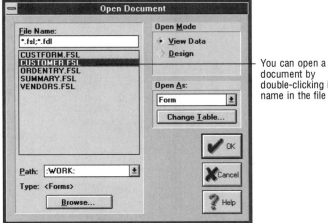

You can open a document by double-clicking its name in the file list

2. Choose CUSTOMER.FSL, then choose OK. CUSTOMER.FSL appears in a Form window and displays the data in your *Customer* table.

When using forms, use the techniques described in Chapter 5 to select different records and fields, edit the field values in the table and locate specific values

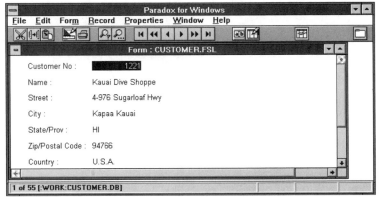

3. To become used to working with forms, repeat some exercises from Chapter 5 using CUSTOMER.FSL instead of a Table window. When finished, close the Form window.

Defining a new quick form

You can design your own form and define it as the quick form by changing the Preferred properties of the table your form is based on.

Example 7-4 Defining a new preferred form

The SAMPLE directory contains a form based on the *Customer* table called CUSTFORM.FSL, shown in Figure 7-1. Suppose you want Paradox to display this form as the quick form for the *Customer* table. To do so,

1. View *Customer* in a Table window. (If you need help, see Chapter 5.)

2. Choose Properties|Preferred|Form. The Choose Preferred Form dialog box appears.

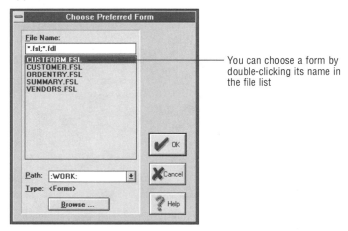

You can choose a form by double-clicking its name in the file list

3. Choose CUSTFORM.FSL, then choose OK.

4. Click the Quick Form SpeedBar button. *Custform* appears instead of the quick form you opened in Example 7-1.

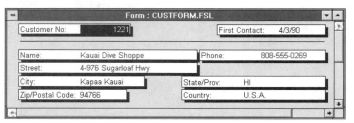

5. Close *Custform* by double-clicking its Control menu. This makes the *Customer* Table window active.

6. Close the Table window by double-clicking its Control menu. Because the preferred form is a table view property, a prompt appears, telling you the properties of *Customer* have been changed but not saved.

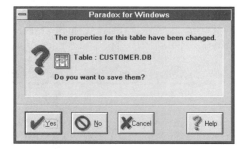

7. Choose No.

Note When you change a table view property, choose Properties I Save to make the changes permanent; otherwise, your property changes are lost when you exit Paradox or close the Table window. If you change your mind about a property change, choose Properties I Restore.

See also For more information about Preferred properties, see Chapter 4 in the *User's Guide*.

Printing forms and reports

Use File I Print to print your design documents and the data they present.

Printing a form

To print a form, click the Print SpeedBar button or choose File I Print while viewing the form. When you do this, Paradox prints the form and the information it currently presents.

Example 7-5 Using a form to print *Customer*

Suppose you want to print the first record in *Customer*, using the design layout of the *Custform* form.

1. Open *Custform* in a Form window. (For help, see Example 7-3.)

2. Make sure the first record is selected. If necessary, click the First Record SpeedBar button (or choose Record I First).

3. Click the Print SpeedBar button. The Print File dialog box appears.

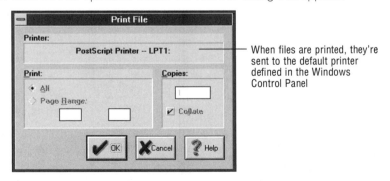

When files are printed, they're sent to the default printer defined in the Windows Control Panel

4. Choose OK to send the form to the printer.

Note You must have a printer driver installed in Windows to print Paradox files. For more information, see your Windows documentation.

Printing the entire table

Forms only print the information displayed on the screen. To print the full contents of a table, use a report.

If you want your report to use the same design layout as a form, open the form as a report.

Example 7-6 Printing a form as a report

Suppose you want to print the *Customer* table using the design layout of *Custform*.

1. Choose Window|Close All to close any open windows.

2. Click the Open Form SpeedBar button to display the Open Document dialog box.

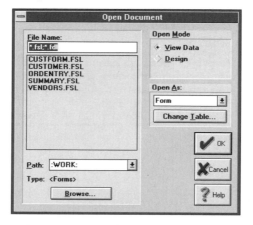

3. In the Open As panel, click the drop-down arrow, then choose Report.

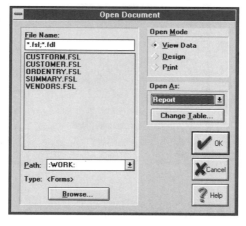

4. In the Open Mode panel, choose Print.

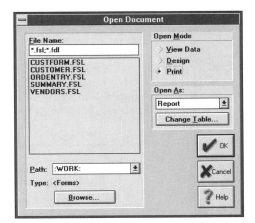

5. Choose CUSTFORM.FSL, then choose OK. The Print File dialog box appears.

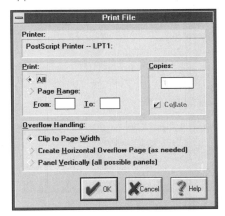

6. Choose OK. Paradox displays a dialog box that tells you the report is being prepared.

Choose Cancel to stop the report before it finishes

7. When the report is finished, the Table window is displayed.

When you open a form as a report, Paradox creates a new report and leaves the original form untouched.

See also For more information about opening forms as reports and reports as forms, see Chapters 12 and 13 in the *User's Guide*.

Printing a quick report

Quick reports let you print a table's data in a tabular format similar to the format of Table windows. To print a table quickly in this format, click the Quick Report SpeedBar button or choose Table | Quick Report while viewing the table you want to print.

Example 7-7 Printing a quick report

Suppose you want to print the *Customer* table.

1. Open *Customer* in a Table window. (If *Custform* is still open, click the Table View SpeedBar button.)

2. Click the Print SpeedBar button to display the Print File dialog box.

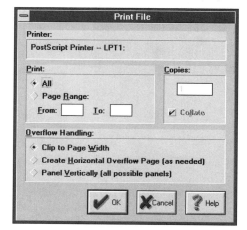

3. Choose OK to print your report.

Printing selected pages

Use the Print panel of the Print File dialog box when you want to print specific pages of a document.

Example 7-8 Printing selected pages of a report

Suppose you want to print the first three pages of the quick *Customer* report.

1. Make sure the *Customer* table is open in a Table window. (If you need help, see Example 5-1.)

2. Click the Print SpeedBar button to display the Print File dialog box.

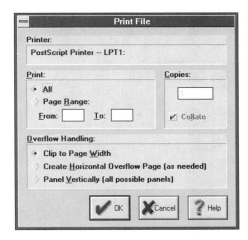

3. In the Print panel, select To, then type **3**.

When you enter a page range, Paradox automatically selects the Page Range radio button —

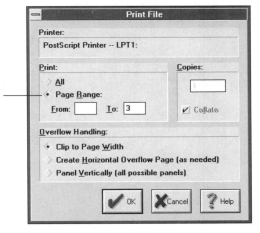

4. Choose OK. Paradox now prints the first three pages of the quick *Customer* report.

Deleting forms and reports

Use File | Utilities | Delete to delete design documents (forms or reports) you no longer want to keep.

Example 7-9 Deleting a form

Suppose you want to delete the *Customer* form you created in Example 7-3.

1. Choose Window | Close All to close any open windows on the Desktop.

2. Choose File|Utilities|Delete to display the Delete dialog box.

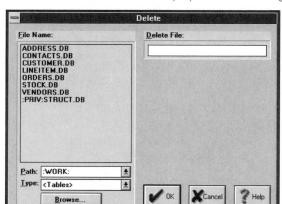

3. Click the drop-down arrow next to the Type text box, then choose <Forms>.

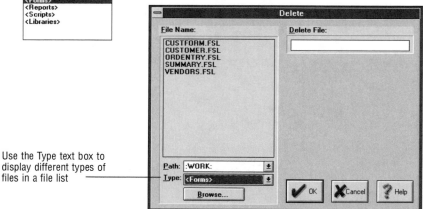

Use the Type text box to display different types of files in a file list

4. Type **customer**, then choose OK. Paradox displays a dialog box asking you to confirm the deletion.

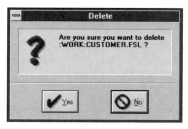

5. Choose Yes. Paradox deletes your file.

CHAPTER 8

Designing new forms

This chapter introduces the Form Design window, which lets you design forms to display, edit and print your tables. This chapter also explains how to

❏ Open and close the Form Design window

❏ View tables using your documents

❏ Select, move, place, and inspect objects in your documents

What is a form?

A form is a design document that displays the data of one or more tables. You can use forms to edit the data in your tables, print specific information, and link tables together. Figure 8-1 shows a form and the objects it contains.

Figure 8-1 A typical form and the objects it contains

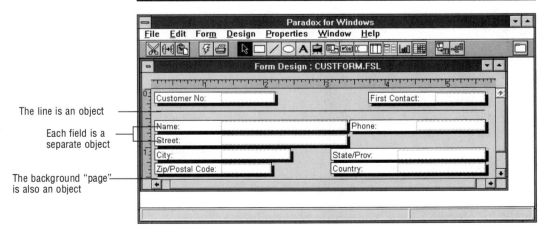

The line is an object

Each field is a separate object

The background "page" is also an object

Creating new design documents

To create a new design document, you need to know the following:

❑ The type of document you want

❑ The table(s) your document will display

❑ The objects your document needs

❑ The way the document's objects should look

Once you've determined these things, create your document:

1. Open a design window for the type of document you want.

2. Place the objects you need on your document.

3. Change the properties of your document's objects so they appear the way you want them.

The examples in this chapter show each step in turn. To learn these tasks, you'll create the form shown in Figure 8-1.

Tip   When designing documents, maximize your Desktop and design windows. This gives you as much room as possible.

See also   For a description of the types of documents you can create in Paradox, see Chapter 7.

Opening a design window

Use design windows to create a new document. To open a new design window,

1. Right-click the SpeedBar button that opens the type of document you want, then choose New (or choose File | New, then choose the type of document you want).

2. Define the *data model* of your document; that is, choose the tables the document will display, then define any relationships between the tables (for example, by linking two or more tables.)

3. Choose an initial layout for the document.

See also   For a full description of data models and how to define relationships in documents, see Chapter 10 in the *User's Guide*.

Example 8-1 Opening a design window for a new form

To create the form shown in Figure 8-1, begin by opening a design window.

1. Make sure you're starting from an empty Desktop. (You can close all open windows by choosing Window | Close All.)

2. Right-click the Open Form SpeedBar button, then choose New to display the Data Model dialog box.

When you add tables to the data model of a
design document, they appear in this panel

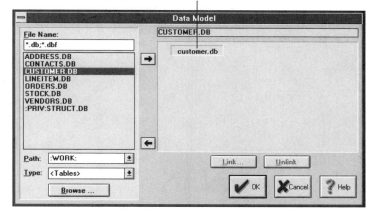

3. Choose CUSTOMER.DB, then choose OK. The Design Layout dialog box appears, which lets you start with different layouts.

These panels let you
choose different initial
layouts

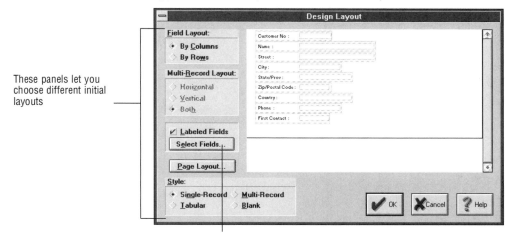

Choose this to remove fields from the initial layout

4. Choose OK. This opens a design window for your new form.

The design window contains the
initial layout you chose in the
Initial Layout dialog box ──────

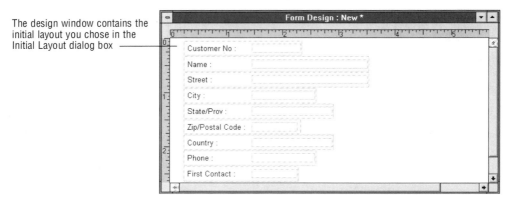

You're now ready to save your form design. This is covered in the next
example.

See also   Chapter 3 in the *User's Guide* describes design windows in detail.

Saving a design document

When you want to save the contents of a design window, choose
File | Save.

Example 8-2 Saving a design document

Suppose you want to save the document you designed in Example 8-1.

1. Make sure you've opened the design window described in Example 8-1.

2. Choose File | Save to display the Save File As dialog box.

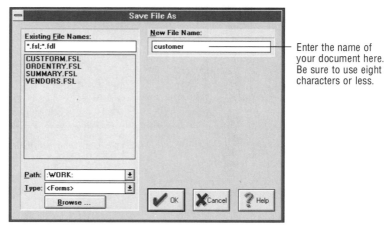

Enter the name of
your document here.
Be sure to use eight
characters or less.

3. Type **customer**, then choose OK. Paradox saves your form as
CUSTOMER.FSL.

To open an existing (or saved) document, click the appropriate SpeedBar button on the Desktop or use the File | Open menu.

Viewing a document

When you want to view your data using a document (or see what your design looks like), do one of the following:

❑ Click the View Data SpeedBar button.

❑ Choose View Data from the document type menu. For example, to view a form, choose Form | View Data. To view a report, choose Report | Preview.

❑ Press *F8*, the View Data shortcut key.

This changes your design window to an appropriate document window. For example, if you're designing a form, the new window is a Form window. If you're designing a report, the design window becomes a Preview window.

Example 8-3 Previewing a document design

Suppose you want to preview the form you saved in Example 8-2.

1. Make sure you've opened CUSTOMER.FSL in a design window, as in Example 8-1.

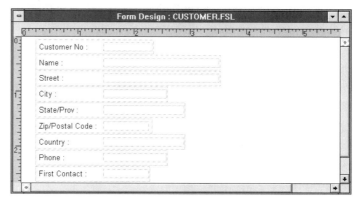

2. Click the View Data SpeedBar button. This changes the design window to a Form window.

The design window
becomes a Form window

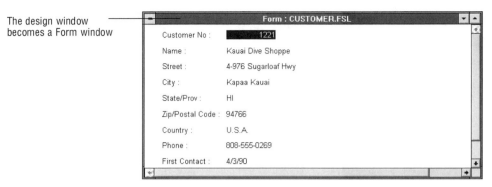

 3. Click the Design Tool SpeedBar button. The Form window now becomes a design window.

Use the View Data and Design Tool SpeedBar buttons to "toggle" your document window and view or change its design.

Working with objects in documents

Paradox uses different types of objects to represent different types of information. For example, Figure 8-1 contains a line, several field objects, and the background page. Each object has properties you can set with the mouse and the Object Inspector.

Selecting objects

Before you can move, change, or inspect an object in a document, you need to select it.

Example 8-4 Selecting objects to change them

Suppose you want to change the text label of the First Contact field object on your *Customer* form.

1. Make sure you've opened the *Customer* form in a design window.

Click an object to select it. 2. Point to the First Contact field object, then press the left mouse button once. When you do this, handles appear in the field object's frame to indicate it is the selected object.

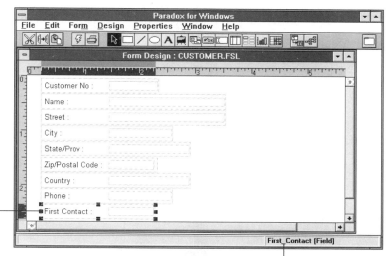

Handles show that
the field is selected ——

Status line message indicates the name of the selected field

3. Point to the text label of the First Contact field, then click the left mouse button once. The handles adjust, indicating you have selected the text label of the First Contact field.

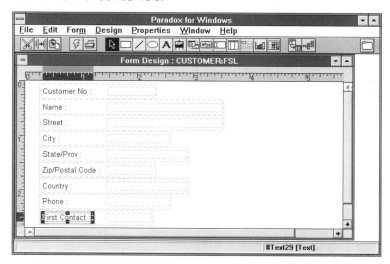

You can also enter Field View by pressing F2.

4. Click the text label to enter Field View and begin editing the text in the label. This places an insertion point in your label, near the place you clicked.

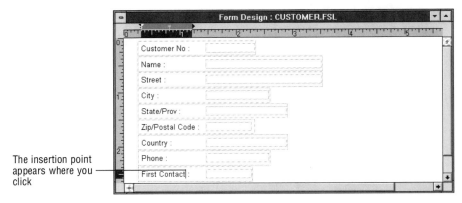

The insertion point appears where you click

5. Press **Home** to move the insertion point to the beginning of the text label.

6. Press **Shift+End** to select all the text in the label.

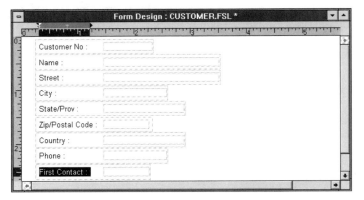

In design windows, Esc selects the object containing the current object.

7. Type **Date Contacted:**, then press **Esc**.

Although you changed the text label, this is still the First Contact field object

8. Press **Esc** again to select the entire First Contact field object.

Containership

As you work with Paradox, it's important to realize that objects are often contained by other objects. For example, the text label you changed in Example 8-3 is a separate object contained by the First Contact field object. To change it, first select the object containing the one you want (the First Contact field object), then select the object you want to change (the text label). This concept is called *containership*. Figure 8-2 describes the contents of field objects.

Figure 8-2 The contents of a field object

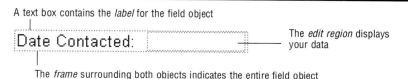

A text box contains the *label* for the field object

The *edit region* displays your data

The *frame* surrounding both objects indicates the entire field object

See also

For a complete description of containership, see Chapter 11 in the *User's Guide*.

Moving objects in documents

To move an object in a document, select it with the mouse, then drag it to where you want it. Use the arrow keys for precise alignment.

Example 8-5 Moving objects in a document

To continue designing the form in Figure 8-1, move the field objects to the places shown in that figure.

1. Make sure you've opened the design window described in Example 8-1.

2. Select the First Contact field object. If you need help, see Example 8-4.

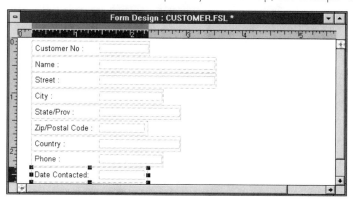

3. Drag the First Contact field object to its new position.

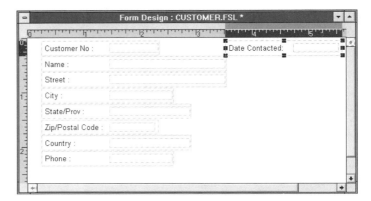

4. Move the other field objects to the positions shown in Figure 8-1. Be sure to leave enough space for the line shown in that figure. (You'll add the line in the next example.)

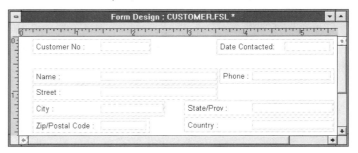

Placing objects in a design document

In design windows, the SpeedBar contains several buttons (called *design tools*) that let you place new objects in your documents, as shown in Figure 8-3.

Figure 8-3 Design tools on the SpeedBar

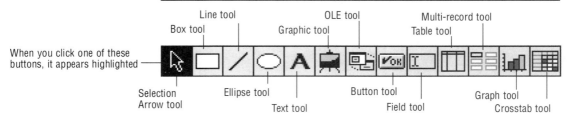

To place a new object in a design document,

1. Click the tool you need on the SpeedBar for the object you want to place in your document.

2. Move the pointer to the place where you want the object to start appearing.

3. Press and hold the left mouse button, then drag the outline to the place where you want the new object to stop.

4. Release the left mouse button.

When you click a design tool on the SpeedBar, the pointer changes to a set of crosshairs next to an image of the design tool you clicked. These pointers are described in Figure 8-3.

Figure 8-4 Design tool pointers

Crosshairs
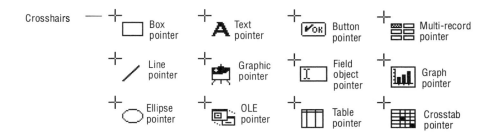

 If you click a design tool by mistake, you can change the pointer back to a Selection Arrow by clicking the Selection Arrow tool on the SpeedBar.

Example 8-6 Placing an object in a document

Suppose you want to add the line shown in Figure 8-1 to your *Customer* form.

1. Make sure you've worked through Example 8-5 and have the *Customer* form open in a design window.

 2. Click the Line tool on the SpeedBar.

 3. Move the pointer so the crosshairs point to a spot between the Customer No and the Name field objects.

4. Press and hold the *left* mouse button.

5. Drag the pointer to a spot below the right edge of the First Contact field object. As you do this, an outline indicates what your line would look like if you released the mouse button.

6. When satisfied with the appearance of your line, release the mouse button. Your form should look like the following figure:

Adjust the size or direction of your line by dragging a handle

Note When designing new documents, save your work periodically. If you make a mistake or if something happens, you won't lose the changes you've made.

Using the Object Inspector

The Object Inspector lets you change the properties of a document's objects. It lets you control the appearance of a document. For example, you can

❏ Change the font used to display a field object

❏ Control the color of an object

❏ Display numbers with different formats and decimal places

Any of these settings or properties can be changed by inspecting the objects on your document.

Properties are characteristics or behaviors of an object.

To change an object's properties, select the object, then inspect it by doing one of the following:

❏ Click the *right* mouse button while pointing to the selected object.

❏ Press *F6*.

❏ Choose Properties | Current Object.

When you inspect an object, a menu appears showing the properties you can change. Choose the property and the settings you want from this menu.

Example 8-7 Changing an object's properties

The form in Figure 8-1 has a gray background. To change your form to look like this example,

1. Make sure you've worked through the earlier examples in this chapter and have the *Customer* form open in a design window.

2. Point to an area of your form that does not contain any other objects, then click the *left* mouse button once to select the page.

Handles indicate you have selected the page

3. Inspect the page by clicking the *right* mouse button once. A menu appears, showing the properties you can set for the page.

4. Choose Color to display the Color palette.

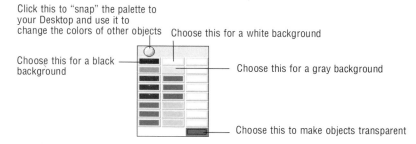

Click this to "snap" the palette to your Desktop and use it to change the colors of other objects

Choose this for a white background

Choose this for a black background

Choose this for a gray background

Choose this to make objects transparent

5. Choose the gray panel. When you do this, all the objects on your form appear in gray, including the field objects. This is because, by default, an object's Color property is transparent; so the color of the page shows through. Continue with steps 6 through 8 to change the color of the field objects.

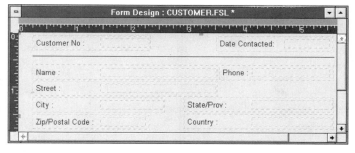

To select more than one object at once, press and hold **Shift***, then click the objects you want.*

6. Select the Customer No object, then press and hold **Shift**.

7. Select the other field objects in turn, then release **Shift**. All the field objects in your form should now be selected.

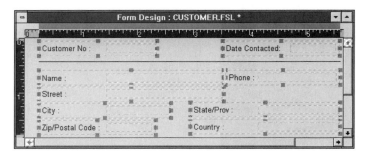

8. Inspect the Customer No field object, choose Color, then choose the white panel. This changes the color of your field objects.

9. Press **Esc** twice. Your form should look like the following figure:

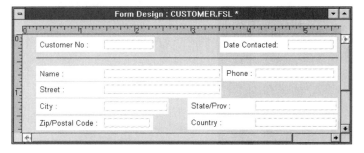

See also   For more information about the Color palette and how it can be "snapped" to the Desktop, see Chapter 11 in the *User's Guide*.

Inspecting more than one object

As you have just seen, Paradox lets you change the properties of more than one object at a time: first, select the objects you want, then inspect one of them.

You can select more than one object at a time in several ways:

❏ Press and hold *Shift*, then click each object you want to change. When you've selected the objects you want, release *Shift*.

❏ To select objects that are near each other,

1. Point to an area above and to the left of the objects you want to select.

2. Press and hold *Shift*.

3. Press and hold the *left* mouse button.

4. Drag the mouse pointer to an area below and to the right of the objects you want to select. As you do this, an outline indicates the area of objects you'll select.

5. Release both the mouse button and *Shift*.

All the objects in your outline are selected.

❐ If the objects you want to select are contained by another object, you can select them by selecting the object containing the objects you want to select, and then choosing Edit | Select All.

Example 8-8 Changing the properties of several objects at once

The field objects in Figure 8-1 appear with a drop shadow. To change the field objects in your form so they appear this way,

1. Make sure you've worked through the previous examples in this chapter and have the *Customer* form open in a design window.

2. Choose Edit | Select All to select all the objects in your document.

3. Press and hold *Shift*, click on the line, then release *Shift*.

4. Press *F6*. This displays a menu of properties you can set for the selected objects.

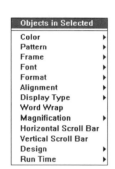

5. Choose Frame | Style, then choose the drop shadow panel.

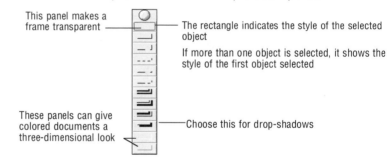

This panel makes a frame transparent ——— The rectangle indicates the style of the selected object

If more than one object is selected, it shows the style of the first object selected

These panels can give colored documents a three-dimensional look

Choose this for drop-shadows

6. Your form should now look similar to Figure 8-1.

7. Save your form (by choosing File | Save), then close it.

See also For more information about selecting and inspecting more than one object at a time, see Chapter 11 in the *User's Guide*.

Tips for designing documents

Paradox has a number of features to help design documents.

❐ The *design grid* helps you size, place, and move objects to specific locations in a document. For example, you can use it to align field objects.

❑ The Design menu lets you

  ❑ Align the edges of objects

  ❑ Control the spacing between objects

  ❑ Make several objects the same size

  ❑ Change the initial layout of a document.

❑ To print a document design, open the document in a design window, then choose File | Print.

❑ If you make a mistake while moving, resizing, inspecting, or placing an object in your document, you can undo it by choosing Edit | Undo.

See also   For more information about these features, see Chapter 11 in the *User's Guide*.

CHAPTER 9

Designing new reports

This chapter explains how reports are similar to and different from forms. It also shows you how to

❏ Create documents containing a selected number of fields

❏ Design reports that *group* related records together

❏ Resize bands

❏ Define *summary field*s

Note   This chapter assumes you've completed the examples in Chapters 7 and 8. If you haven't, do so before using the following examples.

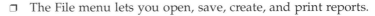

What you already know about designing reports

If you worked through the examples in Chapters 7 and 8, you already know the basics of designing reports. For example,

❏ The File menu lets you open, save, create, and print reports.

❏ The Open Mode panel of the Open Document dialog box lets you control the window that Paradox opens for the report. (Choose View Data to open the report in a Preview window, and choose Design to open it in a design window.)

❏ Design windows let you change a report's design layout and the objects it contains.

❏ The Object Inspector lets you control the way objects look and behave on your reports.

❏ Click the View Data button, choose Report|Preview, or press *F8* to preview a report on the screen.

Creating documents containing a selected number of fields

To create documents containing only selected fields, use the Select Fields dialog box to remove the fields you *don't* want the document to display.

Example 9-1 Creating a document displaying selected fields

Suppose you want to create a report that prints the orders placed by your customers, but don't want it to include all the fields from *Orders*.

1. From the Desktop, right-click the Open Report SpeedBar button, then choose New (or choose File|New|Report) to display the Data Model dialog box.

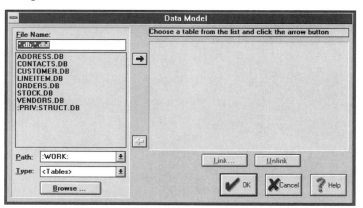

2. Choose ORDERS.DB, then choose OK. The Design Layout dialog box appears.

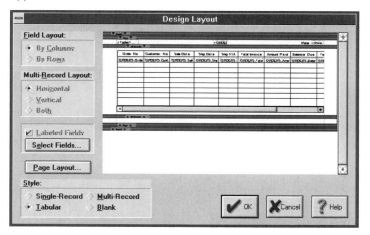

3. Choose Select Fields to display the Select Fields dialog box.

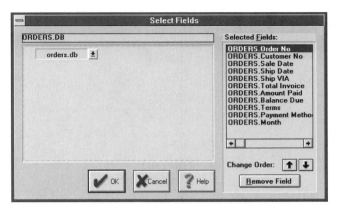

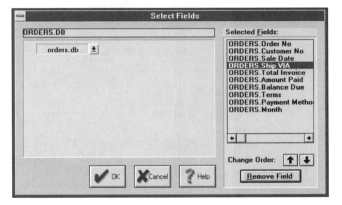

4. In the Selected Fields panel, select ORDERS.Ship Date, then choose Remove Field. This keeps Paradox from including Ship Date in the initial report design.

5. Repeat step 4 for the Ship Via, Payment Method, and Month fields. When finished, your Select Fields dialog box should look like the following figure:

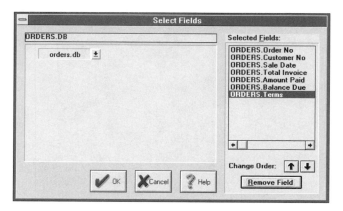

6. Choose OK to return to the Design Layout dialog box, then choose OK to open a design window containing your new report design.

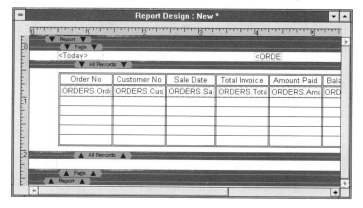

7. Choose File|Save, then save your report as ORDERS.

Tip If you make a mistake while selecting fields, choose Cancel from the Select Fields dialog box. When you return to the Initial Layout dialog box, choose Select Fields and try again.

See also For more information about the Select Fields dialog box, see Chapter 10 in the *User's Guide*.

Report bands

Although reports are similar to forms, they contain *bands* that let you control where and how information appears in the final report. Using bands, you can

❏ Create headers and footers

❑ Separate groups of related records

❑ Summarize totals for groups of records

All Paradox reports contain at least three bands, as shown in Figure 9-1.

Figure 9-1

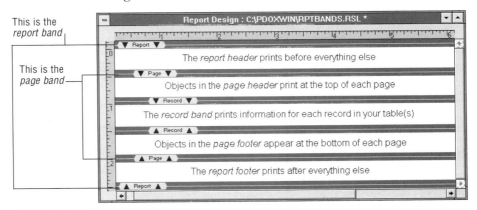

Record band

The record band is the "center" of a report. It prints information for every record in the table(s) the report is based on. For example, if you have 255 records in your table and include field objects in the record band, you see 255 records when you print your report.

Page band

The page band prints information at the top and at the bottom of each page in your report.

To display something at the top of the page (before any record band information appears), place it in the *page header*, the region above the record band.

To print something on the bottom of the page (after the record band information), place it in the *page footer*, the region below the record band.

Report band

The report band (containing the report header and the report footer) prints before and after everything else in the report is printed.

To print something before anything else (a title page, for example), place it in the *report header*, the area above the page header.

To print something after everything else is printed (for example, an index), place it in the *report footer*, the region below the page footer.

Figure 9-2 shows the bands (and their contents) of the *Orders* report you created in Example 9-1.

Figure 9-2

Because the report boundary line touches the page boundary line, there isn't a report header

By default, field objects are placed in table frames in reports

Because the record boundary line *doesn't* touch the page boundary line, there *is* a page footer

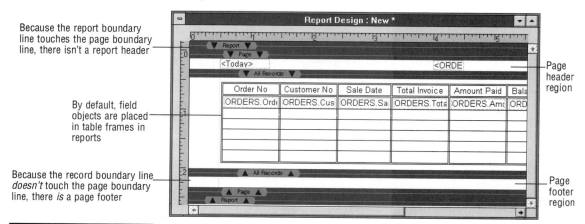

Page header region

Page footer region

Boundary lines

The thick lines separating each region of the report are *boundary lines* and indicate the placement of your report bands. As shown in Figure 9-2, band regions print something (even whitespace) if their boundary lines do *not* touch neighboring boundary lines.

For example, in your *Orders* report, there is no report header because the report header boundary line touches the page header boundary line.

Each boundary line contains a band label with a text description and an arrow pointing toward the report region affected by that line. For example, the arrow in the top page band boundary line points down because the page header is below that boundary line.

Resizing a band

To quickly change the size of a band (and the amount of space it prints), select the band you want to resize, then drag the appropriate boundary line to the size you want.

Example 9-2 Resizing a report band

By default, the page band prints a margin at the top of each page in a report. To increase this margin to one inch (2.54 cm) in the *Orders* report,

1. Make sure you've worked through Example 9-1 and have opened the *Orders* report in a design window. (If you need help, see Chapter 7.)

2. Point to the top page boundary line (the one with the arrow pointing down), then click the left mouse button once. This selects the page band.

The page band is highlighted when you select it

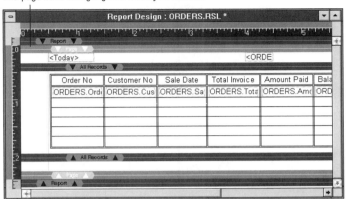

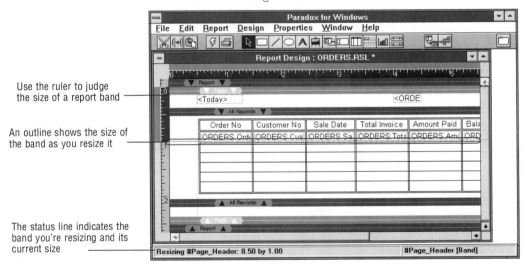

3. Point to the top All Records band line. When the pointer changes to a double arrow, press and hold the left mouse button. An outline appears and indicates where the boundary would appear if you released the mouse button.

4. Drag the pointer (and the outline) to the one-inch mark (2.54 cm) along the left side of the design window.

Use the ruler to judge the size of a report band

An outline shows the size of the band as you resize it

The status line indicates the band you're resizing and its current size

5. Release the mouse button. Paradox lengthens the page header to the new size.

Report bands

When this report is printed, the page header will put one inch of white space at the top of every page, along with the date, table name, and page number objects

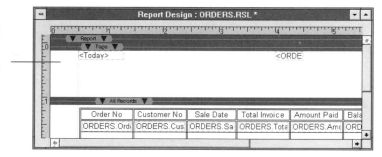

6. Save your report.

See also For a full description of how to resize bands, see Chapter 13 in the *User's Guide*.

Group bands

Paradox supports another type of band called a *group band* that lets you organize your reports in different groups of values without sorting or indexing the table.

Example 9-3 Adding a group band

Suppose you want to change the *Orders* report so it groups orders according to the customer who placed the order.

1. Make sure the *Orders* report is opened in a Report Design window.

2. Press *Esc* to make sure no objects are selected. Do this until there are no highlights in the rulers.

3. Click the Add Band SpeedBar button (or choose Report|Add Band.) The Define Group dialog box appears.

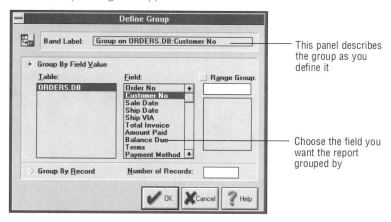

This panel describes the group as you define it

Choose the field you want the report grouped by

4. Choose Group by Field Value. In the Field list, choose Customer No, then choose OK. Paradox inserts the new band in your report design and places a new field object, defined as Customer No (the field you grouped by) in the group's header.

This prints each unique value in the Customer No field when the report is printed —

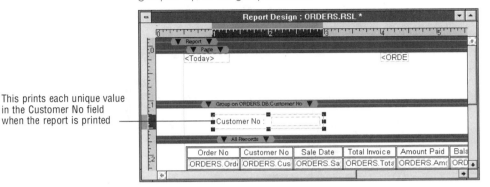

5. Preview your report, then notice how each customer's orders are grouped together. When finished, click the Design tool, then save your report.

Use group bands to separate groups of records from each other and to perform summary calculations.

See also   For more information about group bands, see Chapter 13 in the *User's Guide*.

Defining summary fields in reports

Summary fields let you calculate the sum, count, or average of groups of records.

To define a summary calculation,

1. Place a new field object on the report design.

2. Inspect the new field object, choose Define Field, then press *Enter* to choose the ellipsis (...) command.

Placing a field object

To place a field object on a document, click the Field tool on the SpeedBar, then use the mouse to place it on the document.

Example 9-4 Placing a field object on a document design

Suppose you want Paradox to display the total amount ordered by each customer before it prints that customer's orders.

1. Make sure you've opened the *Orders* report in a design window and that you've stepped through Example 9-3.

Defining summary fields in reports

2. Click the Field Tool SpeedBar button. When you do this, the Selection Arrow pointer changes to the Field Tool pointer.

3. Point to an area to the right of the Customer No field object in the group header, then press and hold the left mouse button. Move the pointer. When you do, an outline shows the size of the new field object, as shown in the following figure:

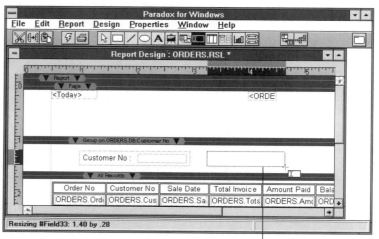

The outline shows the size of the new field

4. Continue to drag the pointer to the right and below the place you pressed the mouse button, then release the mouse button. Paradox places an undefined field object on the report design.

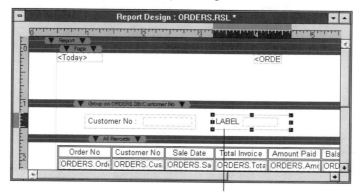

The new object contains a field object, a text label, and a transparent frame object

See also   For information about how Paradox places objects in document designs, see Chapter 11.

Defining a summary field

To define a field object as a summary field, use the Define Field Object dialog box.

Example 9-5 Defining a summary field

To define a summary field,

1. Make sure you've opened the *Orders* report in a design window and have completed Example 9-4.

2. Inspect the field object you placed in Example 9-4, choose Define Field, then press *Enter*. This displays the Define Field Object dialog box.

Click the drop-down arrow to display a list of the fields in *Customer*

This panel describes the summary field as you define it ——

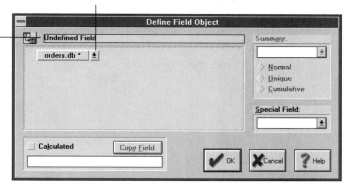

3. Click the drop-down arrow for the *Orders* table, then choose Total Invoice.

4. In the Summary panel, click the drop-down arrow and choose Sum.

Click the drop-down arrow for a list of summary operations

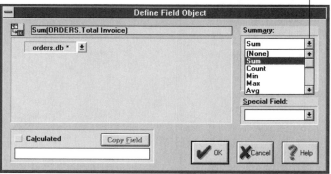

5. Choose OK. Paradox now defines the new object as a summary calculation that totals the invoices for each customer. To verify this, preview the report.

Defining summary fields in reports

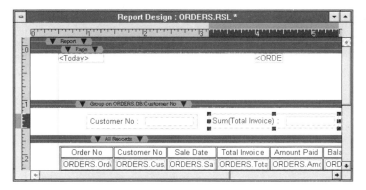

6. After previewing your report, click the Design tool, save your report, then close its design window.

Tip   To change the text that appears to the left of a summary field object, edit the object's text label by clicking it once to select it and a second time to enter Field View. For more information, see Example 8-4.

See also   For more information about using summary fields, see Chapter 13 in the *User's Guide*.

CHAPTER 10

Designing mailing labels

This chapter shows how to create a report that prints mailing labels. It describes what you need to know before starting and how to

❑ Open and define a multi-record report

❑ Set the margins and the page band for labels

❑ Use text objects to "squeeze" (remove) blank fields and lines

❑ Add conditional logic to documents so punctuation in your labels appears only when appropriate

Note The examples in this chapter assume you have read Chapters 7 through 9. Refer to these chapters if you need help.

How to design a mailing label report

Before designing your report, you need the following information:

❑ The table(s) and fields containing the data you want on the labels

❑ Which fields might contain blank values

❑ The size, layout and margins of your printer labels

❑ The height and width of each label

❑ The layout of your printer labels, including how many are printed across each page (for example, how many columns are on the page) and the amount of space separating each label

If your labels do not come with a list of specifications, use a ruler to determine them.

Caution Use mailing labels appropriate for your printer. Although it may be possible to use dot-matrix labels in your laser printer, it's best not to. You may damage your printer by doing so.

Using the examples in this chapter, you'll design a mailing label report with the following specifications:

❑ The report is based on the *Customer* table and uses all of its fields *except* Customer No, Phone, and First Contact.

❑ The City, State/Prov, Zip/Postal Code, and Country fields might contain blank values.

These dimensions match the specifications of laser printer labels commonly available at office supply stores.

❑ The label sheet contains 30 labels (three columns and ten rows) and has half-inch (1.27 cm) margins around the edges of each page.

❑ Each label is 2.5 inches (6.35 cm) wide and one inch (2.54 cm) tall.

❑ There is no vertical or horizontal space separating each label.

Designing the report

Once you have the information you need, design your mailing label report by taking these steps:

1. Open and define a new multi-record report whose data model contains the table(s) and fields you need.

2. Remove the page header and footer.

3. Move and inspect the fields on your report so they appear the way you want.

4. Resize the record region to fit one label and the multi-record region to fit a row of labels.

When designing a report for mailing labels, you can improve the appearance of your labels by

❑ Placing text objects around the fields that might contain blank values

❑ Adding conditional fields that print punctuation only when a field contains a value

Creating a multi-record report

To open a new report as a multi-record report, choose Multi-Record from the Style panel of the Design Layout dialog box.

Example 10-1 Opening a multi-record report

To begin designing your mailing label report,

1. From the Desktop, right-click the Open Report SpeedBar button, then choose New.

2. When the Data Model dialog box appears, choose CUSTOMER.DB, then choose OK to display the Design Layout dialog box.

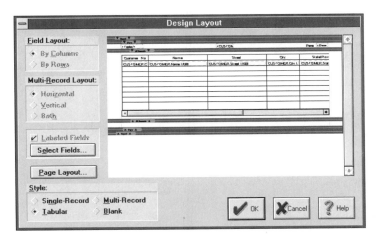

3. In the Style panel, choose Multi-Record by clicking its radio button or by pressing *Alt+M*. When you do this, the sample layout panel shows the new design.

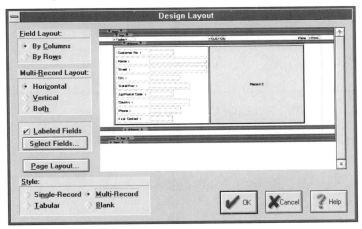

4. Remove the checkmark next to Labeled Fields by clicking it or by pressing *Alt+L*.

Select Fields...

5. Choose Select Fields to display the Select Fields dialog box, then remove the Customer No, Phone, and First Contact fields from your report. When finished, choose OK. (If you need help, see Example 9-1.)

Page Layout...

6. Click the Page Layout button to display the Page Layout dialog box.

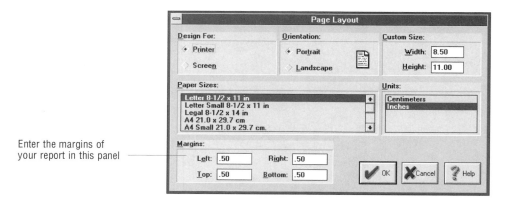

Enter the margins of
your report in this panel

7. Make sure each text box in the Margins panel contains .50, then choose OK to return to the Design Layout dialog box.

8. Choose OK to open the new report in a design window, then choose File|Save As, and save your report as LABELS. (If you need help, see Example 9-1.)

Tip When designing a mailing label report, use Properties|Zoom to adjust the magnification of your report. Use Fit Width to see the width of your report, Fit Height to see how many labels fit on a page, and Best Fit to combine the two settings.

What are multi-record reports?

In Chapter 8, you created a form using a *single record* style to display one record at a time in a vertical list. The report you designed in Chapter 9 used a *tabular* style to display fields in a format similar to Table windows. A *multi-record* report combines the two styles. It displays fields in a list *and* displays more than one record at a time.

When designing multi-record reports, use the *record region* to create the layout for each record, then define the *multi-record region* to contain the number of records you want on each page. Figure 10-1 shows these areas.

Figure 10-1 Record and multi-record regions

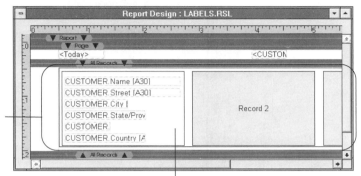

The *multi-record region* contains areas for each record in the record band

The *record region* contains the field objects

Moving the multi-record region

When designing a report for mailing labels, minimize the amount of whitespace in your report design; otherwise, your labels may appear to "creep" when the report is printed. To prevent this, move the record region to the upper left corner of the multi-record region.

Example 10-2 Minimizing whitespace in a multi-record region

To minimize the amount of whitespace used by the record region,

1. Select the multi-record region by clicking it.

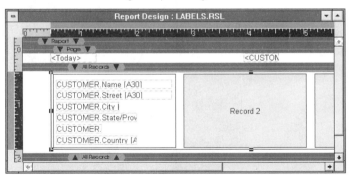

2. Select the record region by clicking it.

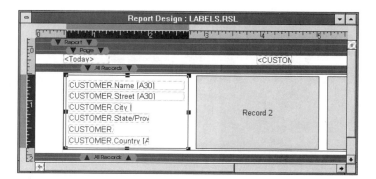

3. Drag the record region to the upper left corner of the multi-record region. When finished, your design should look like the following figure:

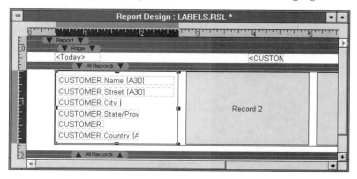

Changing the page band for mailing labels

In Chapter 9, you saw how Paradox places three field objects in the page header of new reports. (These objects print the current date, the name of the table that the report is based on, and the page number.) When designing a mailing label report, delete these objects, then resize the page band so it doesn't add any space to the report.

Example 10-3 Minimizing whitespace in the page band

To remove the default page header and resize the page band so it doesn't add space to the report,

1. Make sure you've opened the *Labels* report you created in Example 10-1 in a design window.

2. Select the page band by clicking it, then choose Edit|Select All. This selects all the objects in the page band:

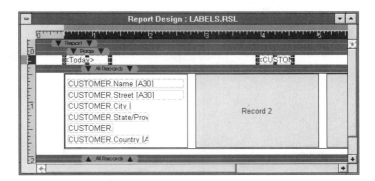

3. Press **Del** to delete the selected objects.

4. Select the page band, then point to the top All Records boundary line. When the pointer changes to a double-headed arrow, press and hold the left mouse button.

5. Drag the boundary line up until it touches the Page boundary line, then release the mouse button.

Page boundary line —

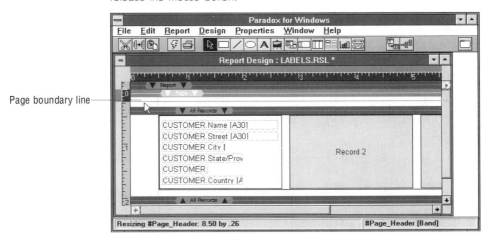

6. Point to the bottom Page boundary line. When the pointer changes to a double-headed arrow, drag the boundary line up until it touches the bottom All Records boundary line.

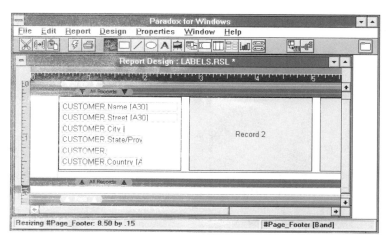

7. Save and preview your report. When you do this, notice that the spacing between some fields is uneven. This happens because some records contain blank fields. The next example shows you how to take care of this.

Using text boxes

To remove whitespace caused by blank fields, place the field(s) that contain blank values in a text box. After you do this, Paradox "squeezes" the blank space when printing or displaying the document.

Example 10-4 Placing text boxes in documents

To squeeze fields that may be blank in your *Labels* report,

1. Make sure you've opened LABELS.RSL in a design window and have performed the earlier examples in this chapter.

2. Click the Text tool on the SpeedBar, then move the pointer so the crosshairs are between and slightly to the left of the Street and City field objects, as shown in the following figure:

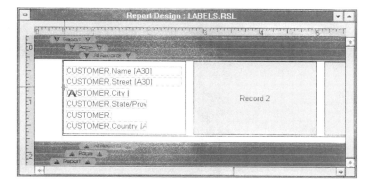

3. Press the left mouse button, then drag the outline until it almost touches the bottom right corner of the record region, as shown in the following figure:

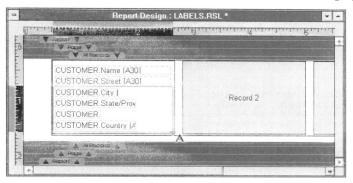

4. Release the left mouse button. When you do this, a text box appears in your report:

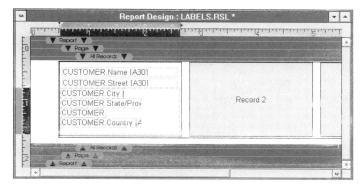

5. Press *Esc*, then choose Edit|Select All to select the four field objects that are now inside your text box:

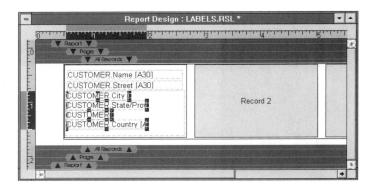

6. Choose Design|Adjust Size|Minimum Width. When you do this, Paradox resizes the selected objects to the same width.

7. Select the text box, then resize it to 0.4 inches (1.02 cm) tall.

When you resize a text box, Paradox reformats the objects inside it to fit the new size—

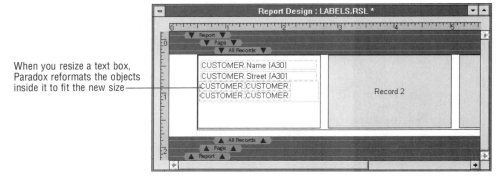

8. Save your report, then preview it. Notice how the field spacing in your labels is consistent, even though some fields are blank. Also, notice that the fields in the text box appear next to each other. To fix this, add punctuation between each field object. This is covered in the next example.

Adding punctuation to a text box

Paradox squeezes fields in a text box so they take up as little space as possible. If two fields are next to each other in a text box, with no space between, Paradox displays the values of those fields right next to each other. To separate fields in a text box, add punctuation and spaces between them.

Example 10-5 Adding punctuation to a text box

To add punctuation between the fields in your text object,

1. Make sure you've opened LABELS.RSL in a design window and have performed Example 10-4.

2. Select the text box, then click it near the bottom right corner. This places the insertion point after the Country field.

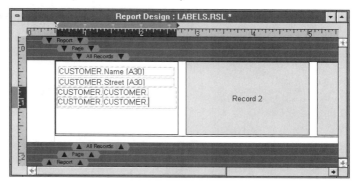

3. Use the arrow keys to move the insertion point between the City field and the State/Prov field, type a comma, then press **Spacebar**.

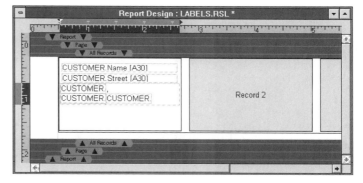

4. Press →, then press **Enter**. Paradox reformats the text box:

Your text box now contains two "paragraphs" (one on each line) because you pressed *Enter* ───

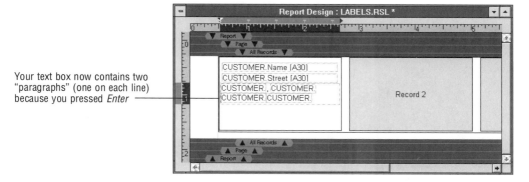

5. Press →, then press **Spacebar** twice to separate the Zip/Postal Code and Country fields. Paradox again reformats the text box:

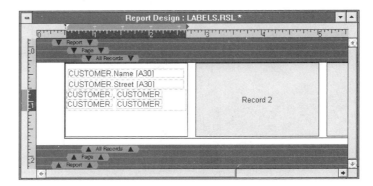

6. Save and preview your report. Notice how the fields in your text box are separated by the punctuation you added.

You're now ready to adjust the report so it fits the mailing labels described at the beginning of the chapter.

Making the report fit your labels

When you've adjusted the fields in your mailing label report so they appear and behave the way you want, you're ready to resize the report so it fits the dimensions of your labels and the sheet they're affixed to.

To do this,

1. Adjust the layout of the record band to reflect the spacing between each label.

2. Resize the record region so it matches the width of one label.

3. Change the height of the record region so it matches the height of one label.

The next three examples show each step in turn.

Note   Before starting this section, make sure the objects in your record region fit within the dimensions of a mailing label. That is, if your label is one inch (2.54 cm) tall, make sure your fields and text object(s) are placed in that area of your multi-record region. If you need to move or resize those objects, use the techniques discussed in Chapter 8.

Changing the spacing between labels

To change the amount of space Paradox places between your labels, inspect the multi-record object, then choose Record Layout.

Example 10-6 Changing the spacing between labels

To resize your multi-record region so no space appears between your labels,

1. Make sure you've opened LABELS.RSL in a design window and have performed the earlier examples in this chapter.

2. Select the multi-record region (by clicking a spot in the shaded box labeled Record 2), inspect it, then choose Record Layout to display the Record Layout dialog box.

3. Select the text box to the right of Separation and below Across, then replace the current value with a zero (0):

4. Press *Tab*, type another zero, then choose OK. Paradox adjusts your multi-record region so there is no space separating its regions:

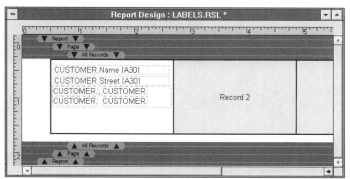

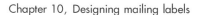

Changing the width of your labels

To adjust the width of your labels, select the record object containing your fields, then drag its right border until it matches the width of one label.

Example 10-7 Adjusting the width of your labels

To make your labels 2.5 inches wide,

1. Make sure you've opened LABELS.RSL in a design window and that your fields are less than 2.5 inches wide. (Use the Horizontal Ruler to check this.)

2. Select the record region by clicking an area that does not contain any field or text objects.

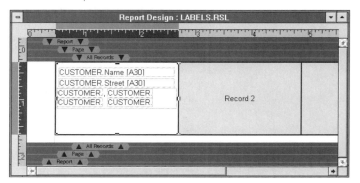

3. Point to the handle in the middle of the right border of the record object. When the pointer changes to a double-headed arrow, drag the handle to the right until the record region is 2.5 inches wide. (Use the status line to check the width.) Your design should look like the following figure:

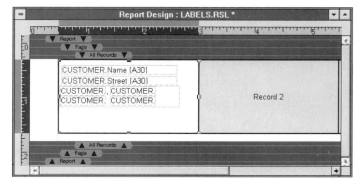

4. When finished, save and preview your report.

Changing the height of mailing labels

To change the height of your mailing labels, select the multi-record region, then drag its bottom border.

Example 10-8 Adjusting the height of your labels

To make your labels one inch tall,

1. Make sure you've opened LABELS.RSL in a design window and that your fields are placed *above* the one-inch mark in the vertical ruler.

2. Select the record region. (If you need help, see Example 10-6.)

3. Point to the handle in the middle of the bottom line of the record region. When the pointer changes to a double-headed arrow, drag the handle up until the record region is one inch tall. (Use the status line to keep track of the current size.)

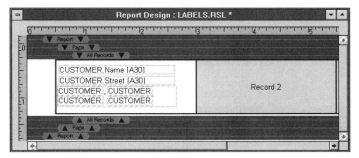

4. When finished, save and preview your report.

Adding conditional logic to documents

Use calculated fields to present information when a specific condition is true. (This is called *conditional logic*.) For example, you can define a calculated field that prints a comma only when there is a value in the City field. This lets you produce professional-looking labels that contain punctuation only when appropriate.

To do this, place an undefined field, then define it as a calculated field. Use the IIF() ObjectPAL function to specify the condition, the result that's printed if the condition is true, and the result that's printed when the condition is false.

Example 10-9 Adding conditional logic to a document

To add the conditional field described above,

1. Make sure LABELS.RSL is open in a design window and that you've completed Example 10-8.

2. Click the Selection Arrow tool on the SpeedBar, select the text box you added in Example 10-4, then place the insertion point between the City field and the comma following it.

3. Press *Del* twice to delete the comma and the space, press *F5* to place an undefined field, then double-click the new field object to select it.

4. Inspect the new field object. Choose Define Field, then press *Enter* to display the Define Field Object dialog box.

#Field25
Define Field ▶
Color ▶
Pattern ▶
Frame ▶
Font ▶
Word Wrap
Alignment ▶
Display Type ▶
Format ▶
Design ▶
Run Time ▶

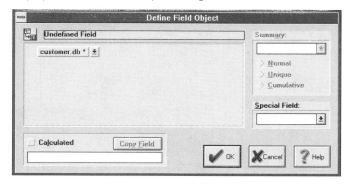

5. Place a checkmark next to Calculated (by clicking it or by pressing *Alt+L*), then select the text box below the check.

6. Type **iif([customer.city] = "", "", ", ")**. (Be sure to type quotation marks, not apostrophes. Also, type a space after the last comma.) This defines the field as a formula that prints a comma and a space if (and *only* if) the City field has a value; otherwise, it returns a blank value and nothing appears on the report when it prints.

This formula prints a comma and a space when City contains a value ——

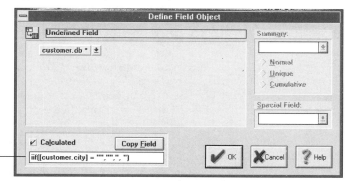

7. Paradox may wrap the fields in your text box. However, Paradox formats the fields correctly when you print or preview the document.

8. Save and preview your report.

Tip You can also use calculated fields to print spaces between fields when appropriate. For example, to print the spaces between the Zip/Postal Code and Country fields only when there is a value in Zip/Postal Code, place and define a conditional field with the following formula: **iif([customer.zip/postal code] = "", "", " ")**.

See also For more details about using calculated fields with Paradox documents (including a list of ObjectPAL functions you can use), see Chapters 12 and 13 in the *User's Guide*.

CHAPTER 11

Querying your data

This chapter introduces queries and shows how you can use them to analyze your data. It explains how to

❐ Open, define, run, and save a query

❐ Use checkmarks to include specific fields in a query's *Answer* table

❐ Perform summary calculations with a query

❐ Limit the records a query works with by using conditions and range values

❐ Join tables in queries with example elements

❐ Change the properties of an *Answer* table before running a query

What is a query?

A *query* is a question you ask Paradox about the information in a table. For example, you can ask questions like

❐ Which customers have placed orders?

❐ What is the total amount of all orders placed by each customer?

❐ What orders have not been paid?

Queries let you locate information, perform calculations, and summarize values in your tables.

Defining and running queries

To define a query,

❐ Open a new Query window

❐ Add the table(s) you want to work with

❏ Enter the actions and conditions you want the query to perform or use

 When finished, click the Run Query SpeedBar button or choose Query | Run.

Example 11-1 Opening and defining a new query

Suppose you want to know which customers have placed orders with your company.

1. From the Desktop, right-click the Open Query SpeedBar button, then choose New (or choose File | New | Query). This opens a Query window and displays the Select File dialog box.

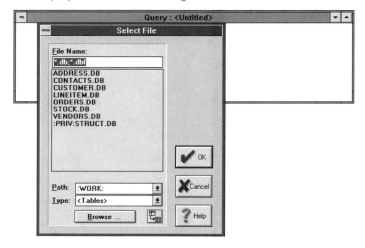

2. Choose *Orders*, then choose OK. A grid representing the fields in *Orders* appears in the Query window:

3. Point to the box in the Customer No field, then press and hold the left mouse button. This displays a checkmark menu, as shown in the following figure:

If you accidentally place a checkmark in the wrong field, clear it by choosing this ————

4. Select the first checkmark, then release the mouse button. Paradox places a *checkmark* in the box. When the query is run, the checkmark tells Paradox to find and display every unique value in the Customer No field.

This shows the
checkmark you placed —

5. Click the Run Query SpeedBar button (or choose Query|Run). When you run a query, Paradox places the results in a temporary table called *Answer*, then opens *Answer* in a Table window, as shown in the following figure:

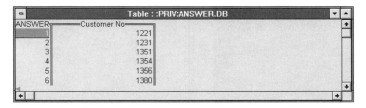

When Paradox runs a query, it leaves the Query window open, so you can return to it to change or save the query. To return to the Query window, make it active by clicking it or choosing it from the Window menu.

Shortcut   To place or remove a checkmark in a field, click its box or select the field, then press *F6*.

What are checkmarks?

Checkmarks limit the records a query works with and tell the query how to handle the results. For example, the checkmark you placed in Example 11-1, told Paradox to include the Customer No field in the *Answer* table then sort *Answer* in ascending order.

See also   For more information about the types of checkmarks you can use in queries, see Chapter 6 in the *User's Guide*.

What is ANSWER.DB?

The *Answer* table, ANSWER.DB, is a regular Paradox table and can be used like any other table. For example, you can edit, print, and restructure it using the techniques discussed earlier in this manual. However, *Answer* is also a *temporary* table, which means it is deleted when you exit Paradox. To keep *Answer* for later use, rename it with File | Utilities | Rename.

Tip   When working with tables that change often, save the query instead of the *Answer* table. To get the latest results, run the saved query.

See also   For more information about temporary tables, see Chapter 6 in the *User's Guide*.

Saving a query

When you define a query, you can save it for later use.

Example 11-2 Saving a query

Suppose you want to save the query from Example 11-1.

1. Make sure you've run the query described in Example 11-1 and the Query and *Answer* Table windows are open on the Desktop.

2. Click the Query window to make it active.

3. Choose File|Save As. This displays the Save File As dialog box:

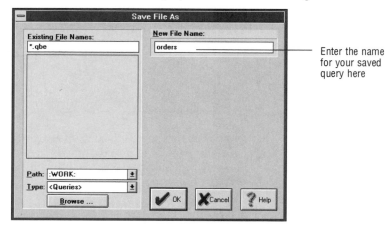

Enter the name for your saved query here

4. Type **orders**, then choose OK.

Paradox saves your query as ORDERS.QBE and stores it in the working directory.

 To open a saved query, click the Open Query SpeedBar button from the Desktop or choose File | Open | Query.

Calculating summary statistics with queries

You can use queries to perform statistical or summary calculations on your tables.

Queries can sum (total), count, and average field values.

Example 11-3 Counting records with a query

Suppose you want to see the total amount that has been paid by each customer.

1. Make sure the query from Example 11-1 is open in an active Query window:

Click the scroll bar to display different fields

2. Click the horizontal scroll bar underneath *Orders* until the Amount Paid field appears.

3. Select the Amount Paid field, type **calc sum all** next to the empty box, then click the Run Query SpeedBar button. The reserved word ALL tells Paradox to include records containing duplicate values in the calculation. After Paradox runs the query, *Answer* displays the total amount, in dollars, paid by each customer.

As you type, the field widens to fit your text. If you want to resize the field manually, drag its right border.

This query tells Paradox to total all amounts paid by each customer, then include (and sort) the customer numbers in *Answer*

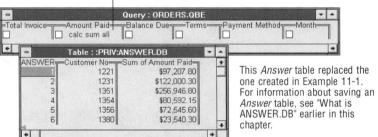

This *Answer* table replaced the one created in Example 11-1. For information about saving an *Answer* table, see "What is ANSWER.DB" earlier in this chapter.

Limiting queries to specific values

To limit a query to specific field values, enter the values into the appropriate field in the Query window. You can also limit queries to a range of values by using range operators, such as > (greater than), < (less than), and other common symbols.

Example 11-4 Limiting queries to specific field values

Suppose you want to know which orders have not been paid.

1. Make sure the query from Example 11-3 is open in a Query window and that the Query window is active.

2. Click the box in the far left column (the one under under ORDERS.DB). This places checkmarks in all the fields in *Orders*.

3. Select the Amount Paid field, then press *Del* to delete the calculation you entered in Example 11-3.

4. Select the Balance Due field and type **> 0** (greater than zero). Your query should look like this:

5. Run the query. When the query finishes, the *Answer* table should look like the following figure:

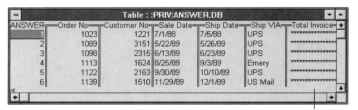

When you see asterisks in a Table window, it means that there isn't enough room to display the value

6. Select a record in the Ship Date field of *Answer*, then press *Ctrl+R*. This feature, called *rotate*, moves the Ship Date field to the end to the table.

You can also rotate fields by dragging their headings with the mouse. For more information, see Chapter 4 in the User's Guide.

7. Rotate the Ship Via field to the end of the table. Your *Answer* table should look like the following figure:

By rotating the fields, you can see how much each customer owes

8. Click the Query window (to make it active), then save your query. (If you need help, see Example 11-2.)

See also For more information about limiting queries to specific field values or ranges of values, see Chapter 6 in the *User's Guide*.

Querying more than one table

Queries can also work with more than one table. For example, you can change the query from Example 11-4 so it displays the names of customers with unpaid orders, even though the names are stored in a different table (*Customer*) than the order information (*Orders*).

Joining tables in a query

In Paradox, tables can be linked (or *joined*) when they have at least one field in common. For example, *Customer* and *Orders* can be joined because they both contain matching values in the Customer No field. That is, every order contains a customer number that matches a number in the Customer No field of the *Customer* table. However, because each table is a separate file, you need a way to tell Paradox how to join them. In queries, this is done with *example elements*.

What are example elements?

Example elements tell Paradox to join tables, by locating common records between the tables.

Naming example elements

You can use any combination of letters and numbers to name an example element, but you can't use punctuation or spaces. For example, EG01, CUSTOMER, X15, and TOWEL are valid names for example elements, but DON'T_PANIC! and EAT@JOES aren't.

What are multi-table queries?

Using example elements, you can define queries that work with up to 24 tables at a time. For example, you can add the *Customer* table to the *Orders* query you saved in Example 11-4, then tell Paradox to display customer names rather than customer numbers. Queries using more than one table are called *multi-table queries*.

To define a multi-table query,

1. Add the tables you want to the Query window.

2. Join them using example elements.

3. Enter the conditions you want to use and the actions you want the query to perform.

The examples in this section show how to add tables to queries and join them with example elements.

Adding tables to queries

To add a table to a query, choose Query | Add Table or click the Add Table SpeedBar button, choose the table(s) you want to add, then choose OK.

Example 11-5 Adding tables to queries

Suppose you want to add the *Customer* table to the *Orders* query you saved in Example 11-4.

1. Make sure ORDERS.QBE is opened in an active Query window.

2. Click the Add Table SpeedBar button to display the Select File dialog box.

3. Choose CUSTOMER.DB, then choose OK to add *Customer* to your query. Your query should look like the following figure:

You're now ready to join *Customer* to *Orders* in your query. This is covered in the next example.

To remove a table from a query, use the Remove Table SpeedBar button.

Joining tables with example elements

To join two tables using example elements (after opening a Query window containing the tables), place example elements using the same name in each of the common fields. To do this, pick a name for your example element, then do the following:

1. Select one of the common fields.

2. Press *F5*.

3. Type the name you want for the example element.

4. Select the other field, then repeat steps 2 and 3 using the same name for the example element.

Use the Join Tables SpeedBar button to do this process quickly. To join your tables, click the Join Tables button, then click the two fields (one in each table) that contain the same values. When you do this, Paradox picks a valid name for your example element and places it in the fields you click in the query.

Example 11-6 Joining tables in a query

In Example 11-5, you added *Customer* to your *Orders* query. To join these tables and tell Paradox to display the customer names instead of the customer numbers when you run the query,

1. Make sure you've added *Customer* to the *Orders* query and that the *Orders* query window is active. (For help, see Example 11-5.)

2. Click the box in the ORDERS.DB Customer No field to remove its checkmark.

3. Click the Join Tables SpeedBar button. When you do this, the pointer, the Join Tables SpeedBar button, and the status line indicate you are joining your tables.

4. Click the Customer No field in ORDERS.DB (the area to the right of the empty box) to place an example element in it. When you do this, Paradox places EG01 in it.

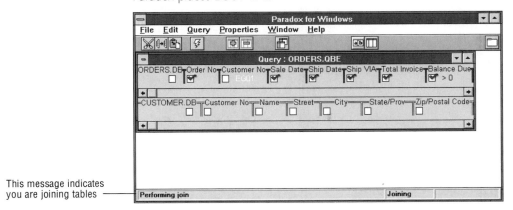

This message indicates you are joining tables —

5. Click the Customer No field in *Customer*. EG01 appears next to the empty box.

6. Place a checkmark in the Name field box of *Customer*.

The example elements in this query tell Paradox: for every value in the Customer No field of *Orders*, perform the calculations, then find a record in *Customer* with the same customer number. The checkmark in Name tells Paradox to include that record's name in *Answer*.

7. Run the query. Your *Answer* table should look like the following figure:

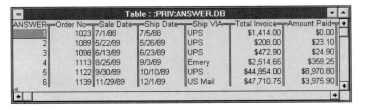

8. To see the Name field, press **End.**

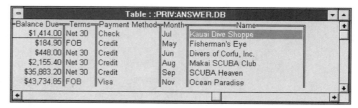

9. Make the Query window active, then save your query.

The next example shows how you can place the Name field next to the Customer No field before running the query.

See also   Chapter 6 in the *User's Guide* describes example elements and multi-table queries in more detail.

Changing properties of the *Answer* table

Use the Properties I Answer Table menu to control the name, table type, properties, and sort order of the *Answer* table before running your query.

Example 11-7 Changing the properties of *Answer* tables

Suppose you want to change the query from Example 11-6 so it displays your customer names after the Order No field.

1. Make sure the query from Example 11-6 is opened in an active Query window.

2. Choose Properties I Answer Table I Options to display the Answer Table Properties dialog box, shown in the following figure:

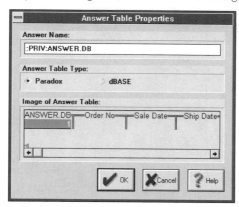

3. Click the scroll bar at the bottom of the Image of Answer Table panel until the Name field appears:

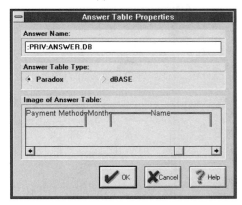

4. Point to the top of Name field. When the pointer changes to a rectangle, press and hold the left mouse button to select the name field. When you do this, the pointer changes to a filled, double-headed arrow, as shown in the next figure:

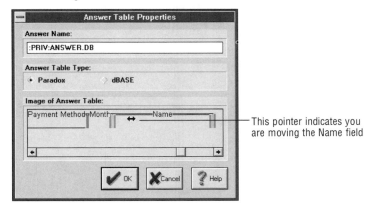

5. Drag the name field until the pointer appears to the right of the Order No field, then release the left mouse button.

Changing properties of the Answer table

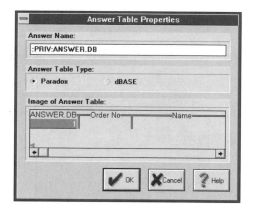

6. Choose OK, then run your query. Your *Answer* table should look like the following figure:

See also   For more information about changing the *Answer* table's properties, see Chapter 6 in the *User's Guide*.

CHAPTER 12

Changing tables with queries

Queries can also change the data in your tables. For example, you can define queries that insert one table's records into another and change a field's values to those in another table. This chapter demonstrates each of these. It explains how to use queries to

❐ Insert records from one table into another

❐ Change a field's values to those in another table

Note This chapter builds on the examples in Chapters 6 and 11. If you haven't completed those chapters yet, do so at this time.

Changing tables with queries

Multi-table queries can copy and change data between tables. For example, you can use queries to fill the *Address* table you created in Chapter 6 with the names from your sample *Contacts* table and the addresses from *Customer*. The examples in this section show how to do this.

Inserting records with queries

INSERT queries are multi-table queries that insert records from one table into another. To define an INSERT query,

1. Open a query containing the "source" table (the table with the records you want to insert) and the "target" table (the table where you want the records to go).

2. Place the INSERT keyword in the left column of the target table.

3. Use the Join Tables button to place example elements in the fields you want to copy from the source table and the fields in the target table where you want your information copied to.

Example 12-1 Defining an INSERT query

Suppose you want to insert the names from the *Contacts* table into the *Address* table (the table you created in Chapter 6). To do this,

1. Close any open windows on your Desktop.

2. Right-click the Open Query SpeedBar button, then choose New to display the Select File dialog box.

New...
Open...

3. Choose ADDRESS.DB, press and hold *Ctrl*, choose CONTACTS.DB, release *Ctrl*, then choose OK. This opens a Query window containing the two tables:

4. Point to the left column of *Address*, then press and hold the left mouse button to display a list of query reserved words:

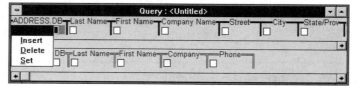

5. Choose Insert, then release the mouse button. This places the reserved word in the field.

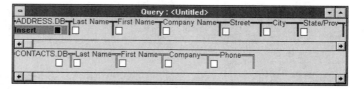

6. Click the Join Tables SpeedBar button, then click the Last Name fields in both tables. Paradox places EG01 in the Last Name fields.

7. Repeat step 6 for the First Name and Company fields in both tables. When you finish, your query should look like the following figure:

Notice that each time you click the Join Tables SpeedBar button, Paradox increments the numbers of your example elements. Because you're working with several fields, different names are given to each set of example elements. This keeps things straight and ensures correct information is inserted in the right field.

8. Run the query. When it finishes, Paradox displays a table called *Inserted*, which contains the records from *Contacts* that were placed in the *Address* table. *Inserted* is a temporary table that lets you recover from a mistake by removing the inserted records. To see the results of your query, open *Address*.

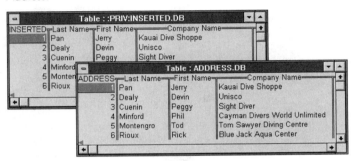

Tip   If you want to insert a table's records into another, and both tables have similar structures, use File | Utilities | Add.

See also   Chapter 6 in the *User's Guide* describes INSERT queries in more detail, and Chapter 8 describes File | Utilities | Add.

Changing records with queries

CHANGETO *queries* let you change the field values in your tables. For example, your *Address* table now contains several blank fields for the addresses of your customers. You can use a CHANGETO query to fill those fields with the values in your *Customer* table.

To define a CHANGETO query,

1. Open the tables you want to work with in a Query window.

2. Use the Join Tables SpeedBar button to link and place example elements in a common field of the tables.

3. Place a new example element in the source field (the one containing the values you want to change your target table to).

4. Select the target field (the field you want to change), type **changeto**, press *Spacebar*, then place the example element you defined in step 3 into the target field.

If you want to change more than one field at a time, repeat steps 3 and 4 for each field you want to change.

Example 12-2 Defining a CHANGETO query

Suppose you want to change the address fields in the *Address* table to the values in the *Customer* table. To do so,

1. Make sure you've run the query described in Example 12-1, then close all open windows on the Desktop. (Don't save the query from Example 12-1.)

2. Open a new query containing the *Address* table and the *Customer* table. (If you need help, see steps 2 and 3 of Example 12-1.)

3. Click the Join Tables Speedbar button, click the Company Name field in *Address*, then click the Name field in *Customer*.

Although the names of the fields are different, they can be joined because they contain the same values

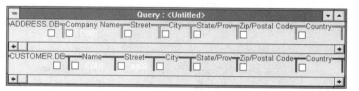

4. Select the Street field in *Customer*, press *F5*, then type **eg02**. This defines a new example element:

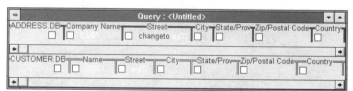

5. Select the Street field in *Address*, type **changeto**, then press *Spacebar*.

6. Press *F5*, then type **eg02**. This uses the example element you defined in step 4.

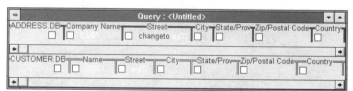

7. Repeat steps 4 through 6 for the City, State/Prov, Zip/Postal Code, and Country fields. Each time, add 1 to the number at the end of the example element. When finished, your query should look like the following figure:

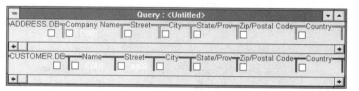

8. Run the query. When Paradox finishes, it displays a table called *Changed*. This is a temporary table containing the records in *Address* that were *changed* (or replaced) during the query. Like the *Inserted* table created in Example 12-1, this is a temporary backup table that lets you return your table to its original contents if you make a mistake.

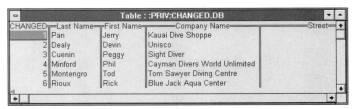

9. To see the results of your query, view *Address*.

See also   Chapter 6 in the *User's Guide* describes the CHANGETO query keyword and the *Changed* table.

Tips for multi-table queries

- ❏ If you make a mistake with an INSERT query using keyed tables, you can return a table to its original condition by using the DELETE reserved word and the *Inserted* table.

- ❏ If you make a mistake with a CHANGETO query, you can return your table to its original condition with a second CHANGETO query that changes your table to the values in the *Changed* table.

- ❏ You can use CHANGETO queries and the BLANK reserved word to erase field values in a table by typing **changeto blank**. (Don't type the period.)

See also   For more information about the INSERT, DELETE, CHANGETO, and BLANK reserved words, see Chapter 6 in the *User's Guide*.

CHAPTER 13

Managing your files

Paradox offers several tools to help you work with your files and directories. This chapter shows you how to use

❐ Folders to display and use the contents of a working directory

❐ Aliases to refer to files located in other directories

❐ The *Browser* button in dialog boxes to locate files in other directories

Tip Because this chapter describes different tools, choose Window | Close All after completing the examples in each section. This will make it easier to complete subsequent examples.

Note The examples in this chapter assume you have installed the ObjectPAL Dive Planner sample application. If you haven't installed these files, see Chapter 2 for information about doing so.

Using folders

The Folder window displays the files in a working directory as icons. This lets you quickly open and use the files in the folder. To open a file in the folder, double-click it. When you do this, Paradox opens the file and performs the file's default action.

Table 13-1 describes icons that appear in a folder, the type of file they indicate, and the default action for that type of file.

Table 13-1 Icons in the Folder window

Icon	File type	Default action
	Tables	Opens the table in a Table window
	Forms	Displays the form in a Form window
	Reports	Prints the report
	Queries	Opens a Query window
	Graphic images	Depends on Windows File Manager
	Text files	Depends on Windows File Manager
	Binary files	No default action

Although graphic images and text files are not Paradox files, they can be opened from a folder. When you double-click one of these icons, Paradox starts the application associated with the file's extension in Windows File Manager, then tells that application to load the file. For example, if you add the README.TXT file to your folder, then double-click its icon, Paradox starts Notepad, then loads README.TXT into that application.

When you exit the application, you're returned to Paradox.

See also For more information about associating an application with a file extension, see your Windows documentation.

Opening the folder

To open the folder for a working directory, do one of the following:

❑ Click the Open Folder SpeedBar button.

❑ Choose File | Open | Folder.

Example 13-1 Opening and using a folder

Suppose you want to use the folder to open the *Customer* table.

1. Make sure you're working in the SAMPLE directory.

2. Click the Open Folder SpeedBar button to open the Folder window. Your Desktop should look like the following figure:

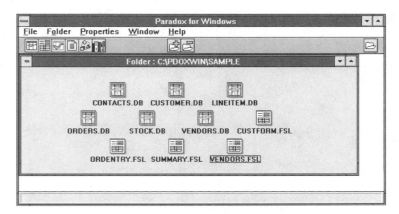

3. Double-click the table icon labeled CUSTOMER.DB to open the table.

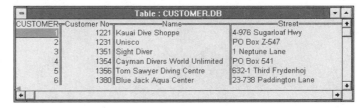

Note When you open a file from the Folder window, the folder remains open but not active. To work with the folder again, make it the active window with one of the following methods:

❑ Click the Folder window.

❑ Choose the Folder window from the Window menu.

To close the Folder window, first make it the active window, then do one of the following:

❑ Click the Open Folder SpeedBar button.

❑ Press *Ctrl+F4*.

Tip Use the folder when you work with several files in a session. This lets you quickly open and use the files.

Adding items to folders

When you first open a working directory's folder, it doesn't contain any icons. To add icons to a folder,

❑ Click the Add Folder Item SpeedBar button.

❑ Choose Folder | Add Item.

❑ Press *Ins*.

Example 13-2 Adding items to folders

Suppose you want to add ORDERS.RSL, the report you created in Chapter 9, to the folder for the SAMPLE directory.

1. Make sure the Folder window is open and active.

 2. Click the Add Folder Item SpeedBar button to display the Select File dialog box.

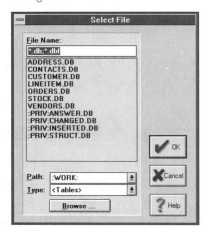

 3. Click the drop-down arrow next to the Type text box, then choose <Reports> to display the reports in the SAMPLE directory.

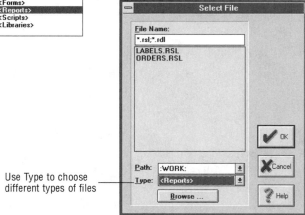

Use Type to choose different types of files

4. Choose ORDERS.RSL, then choose OK. This adds a report icon, labeled ORDERS.RSL, to the folder:

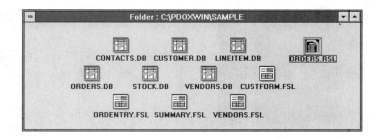

Adding files from other directories

You can also add files from other directories to a folder. This lets you use files located in different directories without changing the working directory. For example, you can add the *Biolife* table, located in the DIVEPLAN directory, then open it while working in the SAMPLE directory.

Example 13-3 Adding files to the folder

Suppose you want to add an icon for the *Biolife* table to the SAMPLE directory's folder.

1. Make sure you're working in the SAMPLE directory, and the Folder window is active.

2. Click the Add Folder Item SpeedBar button to display the Select File dialog box.

3. Type **c:\pdoxwin\diveplan**, then press *Enter* to list the files in that directory. (If you installed the sample Dive Planner application to a different directory, type that directory's name instead.)

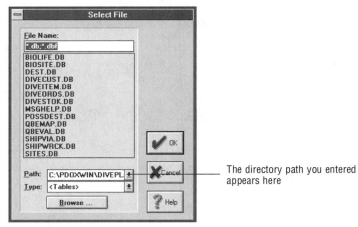

The directory path you entered appears here

4. Choose BIOLIFE.DB, then choose OK to add it to the folder.

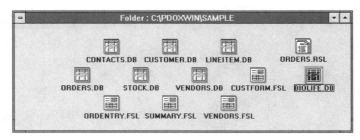

You can now open *Biolife* by double-clicking its icon, even though you're still working in the SAMPLE directory.

 To remove a file's icon from the folder, click the Remove Folder Item SpeedBar button, choose Folder | Remove Item, or press *Del*.

See also Chapter 3 in the *User's Guide* describes folders in more detail.

Displaying an icon's menu

Like the SpeedBar buttons, you can right-click an icon in a folder to display a menu of commands. When you do this, Paradox displays commands appropriate for the file represented by the icon. For example, if you right-click a table icon, you see commands that affect the table. If you right-click a report icon, the menu contains commands appropriate for reports.

Example 13-4 Right-clicking a folder icon

Suppose you want to use the folder to display the structure of the *Customer* table.

1. Make sure you're working in the SAMPLE directory and that the folder is the active window.

2. Right-click the icon for CUSTOMER.DB. This displays a menu of table-related commands:

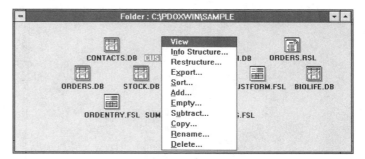

3. Choose Info Structure to display the structure of *Customer*.

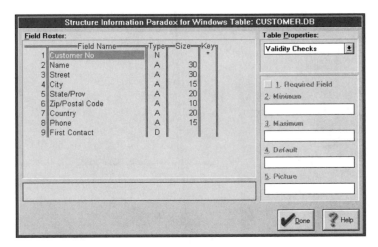

4. Choose Done to close the Structure Information dialog box.

Tip   To delete a design document using the folder, right-click its icon, then choose Delete.

Aliases

An *alias* is a shortcut name for a directory path and lets you refer to files in a directory without typing the full path. For example, you can define :DIVE: as an alias for the directory containing the sample Dive Planner application. You can then open files located in that directory by typing **:DIVE:**, instead of **C:\PDOXWIN\DIVEPLAN**.

Defining an alias

Before you can use an alias, you need to define it. Use File I Aliases to define, keep, change, and remove aliases.

Example 13-5 Defining a directory alias

Suppose you want to define DIVE as an alias for the directory containing the sample Dive Planner application.

1. Make sure you're working in the SAMPLE directory, then choose Window I Close All to close any open windows.

2. Choose File I Aliases to display the Alias Manager dialog box.

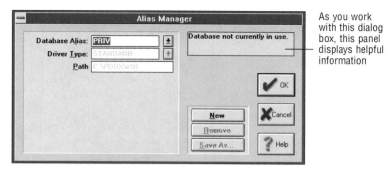

As you work with this dialog box, this panel displays helpful information

3. Choose New (by clicking its button or by pressing *Alt+N*) to add a new alias.

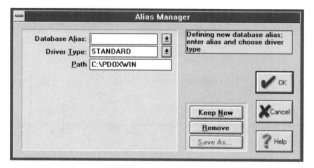

4. Type **dive**, then press *Tab* twice to select the Path text box.

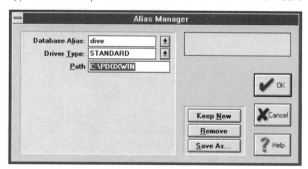

5. Type **c:\pdoxwin\diveplan**. (If you installed the Dive Planner to a different directory, type it instead.)

6. Choose OK to save the defined alias.

Aliases stay in effect until you exit Paradox. To keep them, choose Save As from the Alias Manager dialog box, then save your alias(es) to ODAPI.CFG.

Using an alias

Once you've defined an alias for a directory, you can use it to quickly refer to files in that directory.

Example 13-6 Opening a table using an alias

Suppose you want to open the *Shipwrck* table using the alias you defined in Example 13-5.

1. Make sure you're working with a clear Desktop, and you've performed Example 13-5.

2. Click the Open Table button to display the Open Table dialog box.

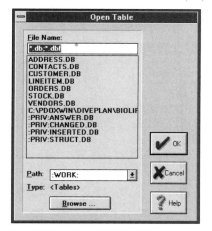

3. Click the drop-down arrow next to the Path text box to display the available aliases.

4. Choose :dive: to display the tables in the DIVEPLAN directory.

5. Choose SHIPWRCK.DB, then choose OK to open it.

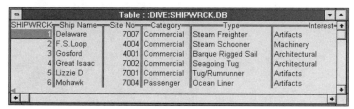

See also For a full description of aliases and how to use them, see Chapter 3 in the *User's Guide*.

Using the Browser

If you can't remember the name of a file, use the Browser to find it.

Example 13-7 Locating a file with the Browser

Suppose you want to open a table in the DIVEPLAN directory but can't remember its name. To find and open it,

1. Make sure you're working in the SAMPLE directory, the Desktop doesn't contain any open windows, and you've defined the alias described in Example 13-5.

2. Click the Open Table button to display the Open Table dialog box.

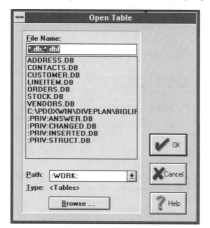

3. Click the Browse button to display the Browser dialog box.

When the Browser dialog box opens, it displays the files in your working directory

To display files in a different directory, click the drop-down arrow of the Aliases text box, then click the directory's alias or drive letter

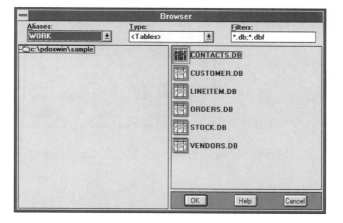

4. Click the Aliases drop-down arrow, then choose dive from the list that appears. This displays the tables located in the alias's directory:

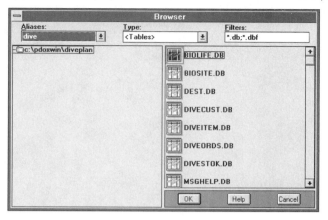

5. Suppose the table you wanted is *Dest*. Choose *Dest*, then choose OK to return to the Open Table dialog box. Notice that DEST.DB is selected:

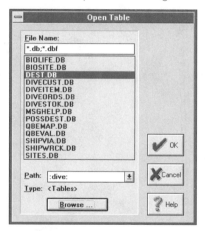

6. Choose OK to open the table.

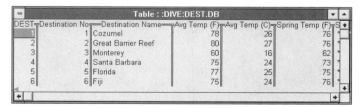

See also   For more information about locating files with the Browser, see Chapter 3 in the *User's Guide*.

Technical topics

This part of *Getting Started* covers technical topics you need to know when installing, starting, and using Paradox in different situations.

Part II contains the following chapters:

❐ Chapter 14, "Configuring Paradox," describes Paradox's configuration files and command-line options and how to use them.

❐ Chapter 15, "Networking Paradox," shows how to install, set up, and use Paradox on a network.

❐ Chapter 16, "International issues," describes the issues you need to know when installing and using Paradox on workstations using non-U.S. settings.

Configuring Paradox

This chapter explains Paradox's configuration files and the options they contain. It describes

❑ The order in which Paradox reads its configuration files

❑ The purpose and settings of each file

❑ How to use the Configuration Utility

❑ The settings Paradox uses from the Windows WIN.INI and CONTROL.INI files

❑ How to override Paradox's configuration settings

❑ Paradox's command-line options

Note The information in this chapter is intended for advanced users. You should understand DOS, Windows, and Paradox.

Paradox's configuration files

When you start Paradox, it reads a number of files to configure the program to your preferences. Because these files are managed automatically, most users will never need to know how they work. However, advanced users and application developers can use these files to control Paradox's behavior.

How Paradox reads its configuration files

The following list shows the order in which each file is read and describes how Paradox uses the file.

1. When you start Paradox, it reads WIN.INI for the location of the ODAPI.CFG file.

2. ODAPI.CFG configures ODAPI and defines the settings that let Paradox work with tables, Windows, and other applications.

3. WIN.INI is read for startup directories and options.

4. PDOXWIN.INI sets the properties and preferences for the Desktop and its windows.

5. PDOXWORK.INI defines settings for the working directory, including the contents of the folder.

Once Paradox is running, it uses two other files for configuration:

❏ DEFAULT.DB (or DEFAULT.DBF) sets the default properties of Table windows. For more information, see Chapter 4 in the *User's Guide*.

❏ PXTOOLS.FT defines the default properties of document design objects. For more information, see Chapter 11 in the *User's Guide*.

ODAPI.CFG

ODAPI lets Paradox share tables and files with other ODAPI-hosted applications, such as the Database Desktop in Quattro Pro for Windows.

ODAPI.CFG tells Paradox how to work with other applications and how to sort your tables.

The ODAPI.CFG file includes these settings:

❏ *Network Control File* specifies the location of PDOXUSRS.NET, the file that controls access to Paradox tables among different applications and users.

For more information about using Paradox on a network, see Chapter 15.

❏ *System Language Driver* defines how Paradox converts ANSI characters to OEM characters when saving tables.

For more information about character conversion, see Chapter 16.

❏ *Paradox Language Driver* lets you select a sort order for Paradox tables only. This can be different from your System Language driver.

❏ *dBASE Language Driver* lets you select a sort order for dBASE tables only. This can also be different from your System Language driver.

For more information about language drivers, see Chapter 16.

❏ *Buffer Size* lets you define the amount of memory (RAM) Paradox uses for table data. It contains three settings:

  ❏ *Minimum* is the smallest amount of RAM (in KB) Paradox reserves for table data. This can be any integer greater than 32 and less than (or equal to) your maximum buffer size.

  ❏ *Maximum* is the highest amount of memory you want Paradox to use. This can be any integer up to the total amount of *extended* memory available on your workstation.

□ *Local Share* indicates whether Paradox should perform network-style table locking on a local hard disk. Turn Local Share on if you want to run Paradox while other applications (for example, Paradox 4.0, ObjectVision, or Quattro Pro) are running on the same workstation. (You do not need to turn Local Share on to run with other ODAPI-hosted applications, such as the Database Desktop in Quattro Pro for Windows.)

See also Chapter 2 describes ODAPI in more detail and tells you when you might need Local Share.

Configuration Utility

To change the settings in ODAPI.CFG, run the Configuration Utility (by double-clicking its icon in Program Manager). When you do this, the dialog box shown in Figure 14-1 appears.

Figure 14-1 The ODAPI Configuration Utility dialog box

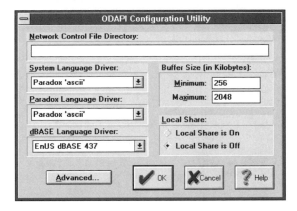

To change a setting, select the option you want, then enter its new value. When finished, choose OK to save your changes. To exit without saving your changes, choose Cancel or press *Esc*.

Advanced settings

The ODAPI Configuration Utility contains an Advanced button that lets you directly configure your ODAPI drivers. This button is for *advanced users only*. For more information, see the online Help system of the Configuration Utility.

Notes for configuring ODAPI.CFG

When configuring ODAPI.CFG, keep the following points in mind:

□ If you configure ODAPI.CFG while Paradox (or another ODAPI-hosted application) is running, your changes do not take effect until you exit all ODAPI-hosted applications and restart one.

□ If you want to share tables and files with other users and applications, set Network Control File Directory to a directory that can be found by all users and applications. If you are not connected to a network, this can be a directory on your hard disk; however, if you are using a network, set this to a network directory.

Be sure to use the same directory for all applications that use PDOXUSRS.NET as the control file, such as Paradox 4.0 and Quattro Pro for Windows. If you set this to a network directory, you *must* have full access rights (create, read, write, and delete) to the directory.

Extended memory is the amount of memory beyond 1MB. For example, if you have 4MB of RAM on your workstation, you have 3MB of extended memory.

❐ For best performance, set the minimum buffer size to $1/3$ of your available extended memory and the maximum buffer size to $2/3$ of your available extended memory. For example, if you have 4MB of RAM installed on your workstation, set Minimum to 1024 and Maximum to 2048.

Available memory is the amount of memory usually available to Paradox. For example, if you have a 4MB workstation and you reserve 1MB of extended memory for a disk cache (for example, SMARTDRV.EXE), you have 2MB of available extended memory. (Remember that DOS uses 1MB of RAM.)

For more information, see your DOS and Windows manuals.

❐ If you want to run Paradox while other applications are running on your workstation, you may need to experiment with your Buffer Size settings to find the best performance settings. Be sure to leave enough memory for your other applications.

❐ If you turn Local Share on, you *must* load SHARE before starting Windows *and* specify a directory for the network control file; otherwise, error messages will result.

Caution   Because Local Share forces Paradox to perform network locking on a local disk, do not turn it on unless necessary; otherwise, performance may suffer.

WIN.INI

WIN.INI contains two sections used by Paradox: [PDOXWIN] and [ODAPI].

[PDOXWIN] contains the following startup options:

❐ *WORKDIR* indicates the last working directory used in Paradox. If you installed Paradox on a local (non-network) drive, this defaults to a WORKING directory below your Paradox system directory, for example, C:\PDOXWIN\WORKING.

❐ *PRIVDIR* specifies the directory where Paradox stores temporary tables, such as ANSWER.DB. If you installed Paradox on a local (non-network) drive, this defaults to a PRIVATE directory below your Paradox system directory, for example, C:\PDOXWIN\ PRIVATE.

❐ *FLAGS* contains default command-line options that override Paradox's normal startup behavior. (This setting must be added manually. For more information, see "Setting permanent command-line options" later in this chapter.)

Paradox updates the [PDOXWIN] section when you exit the program.

See also For more information about working and private directories, see Chapter 15.

[ODAPI] contains settings that tell ODAPI the name and location of its configuration files, usually C:\WINDOWS\SYSTEM\ODAPI.CFG. This section may contain settings from other ODAPI-hosted applications, like Database Desktop. The setting for Paradox is CONFIGFILE01.

Caution Use care when changing CONFIGFILE01. If you include a directory path, but not a file name, Paradox assumes you want it to look for ODAPI.CFG in the directory you indicated.

Note If you change WIN.INI while Windows is running, you must exit and restart Windows for your changes to take effect.

PDOXWIN.INI

PDOXWIN.INI describes the Desktop, its properties, and its windows. It contains the following sections:

❐ *[Desktop]* configures the appearance of the Desktop. It describes the position, size and state of the Desktop. To change these in Paradox, use the mouse to move or resize the Desktop.

❐ *[Windows]* describes any windows that were open the last time you exited Paradox. The settings in this section describe the file that was open, the Paradox module that was using it, and the properties of the window containing the file.

❐ *[Properties]* contains the property settings of the Desktop, including the message displayed in the title bar, the background bitmap, and the settings of the SpeedBar. Use the Properties | Desktop command to change these settings in Paradox.

❐ *[Designer]* contains options chosen from the Designer Properties dialog box.

PDOXWIN.INI can also contain a section listing preferences for each window in Paradox. These sections appear when you save a window's defaults from the Properties menu. For example, if you change the grid while designing a form and then choose Properties | Form Options | Save Defaults, your changes appear in a [Form] section.

The settings in these window-specific sections vary, depending on the window being described. Some common settings in these sections include the following:

❏ *RulerVert*, *RulerHoriz*, and *RulerExtd* indicate whether or not the vertical, horizontal, and extended rulers are displayed.

❏ *Grid* indicates whether or not Properties | Show Grid is selected.

❏ *GridSnap* is the setting for Snap to Grid.

❏ *Zoom* indicates the level of magnification used to display a document in a window.

See also For a complete list of the settings found in PDOXWIN.INI, see the SETTINGS.TXT file in the online Help system.

PDOXWORK.INI

PDOXWORK.INI describes a working directory's folder. The *[Folder]* section indicates the files in the folder, each file's type, and the positions of the icons.

You can use PDOXWORK.INI to override settings in PDOXWIN.INI. For further details, see "Overriding Paradox's configuration settings" later in this chapter.

How Windows Control Panel affects Paradox

Because Paradox is a Windows application, it inherits many configuration settings from Windows itself, including

❏ Default colors used for windows and menus

❏ Printer information

❏ Your network type, if any

❏ International settings for documents and table properties, such as keyboard type, decimal indicator, and thousands separator

❏ The formats and values of the system DATE and TIME variables

These values are saved in Windows .INI files. To change them, use Control Panel.

You should be familiar with these settings because Paradox uses them for workstation-specific defaults when displaying tables, forms, and reports. For example,

❏ If Windows doesn't know that your printer supports a landscape mode, neither does Paradox.

❏ By default, Paradox displays number and date values using the formats defined in Control Panel. That is, if your copy of Windows uses two decimal places to display numbers, so will

Paradox. Similarly, if Windows displays dates in MM/DD/YY format, Paradox will too.

Tip   If a table looks different on different workstations, make sure Control Panel has the same settings for each workstation and that both tables are using the same Format property settings.

See also   For information about using Paradox in an international (non-U.S.) setting, see Chapter 16.

Overriding Paradox's configuration settings

Paradox saves configuration settings to different .INI files. You can override the settings in these files by either

❐   Placing specific settings in PDOXWORK.INI to override settings in PDOXWIN.INI

❐   Specifying an alternate file using command-line options

Caution   Before attempting to override Paradox's .INI files, make a backup copy of all .INI files used by Paradox. Should something go wrong, you will be able to return to your earlier settings.

Overriding specific configuration settings

Using a text editor (like Notepad), you can add sections and settings to PDOXWORK.INI that override the settings in PDOXWIN.INI. This is useful for developers who want to "force" applications to use specific settings.

For example, to always display the grid when designing forms in the SAMPLE directory (regardless of the settings in PDOXWIN.INI), add a [Form] section containing Grid=On to the PDOXWORK.INI file in SAMPLE. Example 14-1 demonstrates one way to do this.

Example 14-1   Overriding Paradox's configuration settings

To make the grid change described above,

1. Start Paradox and change your working directory to the SAMPLE directory.

2. Open a form in a Design window and make sure Properties | Show Grid does not have a checkmark next to it. (If you need to change this, choose Properties | Form Options | Save Defaults when finished.)

3. Exit Paradox, then start Notepad. (Do *not* use *Alt+Esc* or *Alt+Tab* to go to Program Manager; these keys switch to Program Manager without exiting Paradox.)

4. Open PDOXWIN.INI, then locate the *[Form]* section. PDOXWIN.INI can be found in the directory that contains WIN.INI (usually C:\WINDOWS.)

5. Copy the entire *[Form]* section to the Clipboard, then close PDOXWIN.INI *without* saving any changes.

6. Open the PDOXWORK.INI file in your SAMPLE directory, move the insertion point to the end of the file, then press *Enter*.

7. Paste the *[Form]* section into PDOXWORK.INI, then delete all the lines except for [Form] and Grid=Off.

8. Replace the word "Off" with "On," save your changes, then exit Notepad.

If you start Paradox and open a form in a Design window, the grid appears (despite the Grid=Off setting in PDOXWIN.INI). However, if you design a form in the DIVEPLAN directory, the grid does not appear until you choose Properties | Show Grid.

Settings placed in PDOXWORK.INI only affect the settings used in the directory containing the modified PDOXWORK.INI. When you change working directories, Paradox uses a different PDOXWORK.INI.

Caution   Do *not* attempt to modify ODAPI.CFG, DEFAULT.DB, DEFAULT.DBF, or PXTOOLS.FT with a text editor. This can damage your copy of Paradox and the data in your tables. These files can be changed *only* with the tools provided with Paradox.

Note   When adding sections to configuration files, be sure to copy the section and setting names exactly as they appear in the original file (for example, [Form] and Grid=On); otherwise, unexpected results might occur.

See also   For a complete list of the settings in Paradox's configuration files, see the SETTINGS.TXT file in your Paradox system directory.

Specifying alternate configuration files

You can override configuration file settings by specifying an alternate file with a command-line option. For example, you can specify an alternate ODAPI.CFG file when you are having network troubles.

Table 14-1 shows the options that let you specify alternate configuration files.

Table 14-1 Command-line options that specify alternate configuration files

Option	Description
-d *Filename* *	Specifies an alternate PDOXWORK.INI file
-i *Filename*	Specifies an alternate PDOXWIN.INI file
-o *Filename*	Specifies an alternate ODAPI.CFG file

* *Filename* is the name of the alternate file to use and must include the file extension.

Example 14-2 Specifying an alternate .CFG file

Suppose your ODAPI.CFG file places the network control file in
G:\PDOXDATA and you have an alternate ODAPI.CFG file called
NONET.CFG, which does not indicate a network control directory. To use
NONET.CFG instead of ODAPI.CFG,

1. Make sure you are not running any ODAPI-hosted applications.

2. From the Program Manager, choose File l Run.

3. When the Run dialog box appears, type **pdoxwin -o nonet.cfg**.

To create an alternate configuration file, copy an existing one using
Windows File Manager or the DOS COPY command.

See also For a complete description of Paradox's command-line options, see
"Command-line configuration" later in this chapter.

How Paradox locates alternate configuration files

Use care when indicating alternate configuration files. What you type
directly affects how Paradox locates the alternate file. The following
list describes how Paradox finds alternate configuration files:

❐ If you type a drive letter, directory path, and file name (for
example, C:\WINDOWS\INIFILES\MYWORK.INI), Paradox
looks for your file in that location.

❐ If you specify a directory path, and file name (for example,
\WINDOWS\INIFILES\MYWORK.INI), Paradox searches the
current drive for the directory and file you indicate.

❐ If you use a relative directory and file name (for example,
INIFILES\MYWORK.INI), Paradox tries to find the directory and
file from the point of view of the working directory. For example,
if the working directory is C:\PDOXWIN, Paradox tries to load
C:\PDOXWIN\INIFILES\MYWORK.INI; however, if the working
directory is C:\, Paradox tries to load C:\INIFILES\
MYWORK.INI.

❐ If you include a file name only (for example, MYWORK.INI),
Paradox searches the working directory for the file.

❐ If you indicate a directory path only (with or without the drive
letter), Paradox looks for the original file name (for example,
PDOXWORK.INI) in that directory.

If Paradox can't locate an alternate configuration file, it uses the
original one. For example, if you use the **-d** command-line option to
tell Paradox to use C:\WINDOWS\INIFILES\MYWORK.INI and
Paradox can't find the file, it uses the PDOXWORK.INI file in your
working directory.

Tip   For best results, always specify the complete location of the alternate configuration file, including drive letter, directory path, file name, and extension.

Creating an alternate configuration file

To create an alternate configuration file,

1. Copy the current configuration file to a backup file using Program Manager or the DOS COPY command.

2. Change the current settings to the settings you want. Use a text editor to change PDOXWIN.INI and PDOXWORK.INI. Use the Configuration Utility to change ODAPI.CFG. Save your changes.

3. Rename the changed file to the name you want using Program Manager or the DOS RENAME command.

4. If you want to use the original file at any time, restore it by copying the backup file to the original name.

Command-line configuration

As the previous section states, Paradox has several command-line options that let you control its configuration. This section describes each command-line option and how to use it.

Table 14-2 describes Paradox's command-line options.

Table 14-2 Paradox command-line options

Option	Description
-c	Starts Paradox with a clear Desktop
-d *Filename* *	Specifies an alternate PDOXWORK.INI file
-i *Filename*	Specifies an alternate PDOXWIN.INI file
-m	Loads Paradox as a minimized application
-o *Filename*	Specifies an alternate ODAPI.CFG file
-p *Directory* **	Specifies an alternate private directory
-q	Starts Paradox without displaying the title screen
-w *Directory*	Specifies the initial working directory
StartFile ***	Opens a document and performs its default action

* *Filename* is the name of the alternate file to use and must include the file extension.

** *Directory* is the directory you want to use for this option.

*** *StartFile* is the name of any Paradox document and must include the file extension.

The following list describes each command-line option:

❏ Use **-c** to start Paradox with a clear Desktop. Normally, when you exit Paradox, it saves the state of any open windows, then reopens them the next time you start the program. If, for some reason, you cannot start Paradox (because a file is missing or corrupted), use **-c** to start without opening windows from the previous session.

❏ Use **-d** to specify an alternate PDOXWORK.INI file with the *Filename* parameter. This lets you create different folders for different users.

If you specify a full directory path (for example, one that includes a drive letter and directory name like C:\WINDOWS\INIFILES) with *Filename*, Paradox uses that file for every working directory you use. However, if you do not include a directory reference and you change your working directory after starting Paradox, then Paradox looks for *Filename* in the new directory. If the file can't be found, Paradox uses the new directory's PDOXWORK.INI.

If Paradox can't find the alternate file, it uses the PDOXWORK.INI for the working directory.

❏ Use **-i** to indicate an alternate PDOXWIN.INI file. If you start with a different file and save settings that are normally written to PDOXWIN.INI, the new settings are written to the file you specified with *Filename*—not to PDOXWIN.INI.

❏ Use **-m** to load Paradox as a minimized application. This is useful if you want to load Paradox but not work with it immediately.

❏ Use **-o** to specify an alternate ODAPI.CFG file. See Example 14-2 for more information. (Remember that all ODAPI-hosted applications *must* use the same ODAPI.CFG file.)

❏ Use **-p** to start with a different private directory from the default. When you use this option, Paradox stores its temporary tables in the directory you indicate with the *Directory* parameter.

If you don't indicate a full directory path (one with a drive letter), Paradox looks for the new directory with respect to the Paradox system directory.

❏ Use **-q** to hide the title screen while Paradox is loading.

❏ Use **-w** to start Paradox with a specific working directory instead of the one saved in WIN.INI.

❏ You can tell Paradox to open a file when starting (for example, a table, form, or report) by typing the name of the file, along with any necessary directory information. This does not require a special option, but does require the file extension. After loading, Paradox opens the file and performs its default action. For example, tables are opened in a Table window, forms are displayed in a Form window, and queries appear in the Query window.

Tip   You can also start Paradox as a minimized application by holding *Shift* while double-clicking the Paradox icon in Windows Program Manager.

See also   For more information about the default actions of Paradox files, see Chapter 13.

Starting Paradox with command-line options

To start Paradox with one or more command-line options, choose File | Run from the Windows Program Manager, type **pdoxwin**, add the option(s) you want to use, then choose OK. If you use more than one option, separate each with a space.

Note   If your DOS path does not contain Paradox's system directory, you need to type it when using File | Run to start Paradox. For example, if Paradox is located in C:\PDOXWIN, type **c:\pdoxwin\pdoxwin**.

Setting permanent command-line options

If you want Paradox to always start with the same command-line options and parameters, do either of the following:

❏ Use Windows Program Manager to change the File | Properties of your Paradox icon.

❏ Create a new icon in your Paradox for Windows Group containing the command-line options in its File | Properties settings.

❏ Use a text editor to add the FLAGS= line to the *[PDOXWIN]* section of your WIN.INI file. For more information, see the SETTINGS.TXT file in your Paradox system directory.

CHAPTER 15

Networking Paradox

The instructions in this chapter are for a network administrator or supervisor—someone with full, or "parental," rights to all directories on the network.

This chapter covers

❏ Types of Paradox network configurations

❏ The network concepts you should understand before you install Paradox for sharing data on a network

❏ The directory structure of each Paradox network configuration

❏ The installation and configuration steps for installing Paradox on a network

Paradox network configurations

You can install Paradox in one of three configurations for sharing data on a network. This section lists these configurations in order from fastest to slowest performance speed and from most expensive to least expensive.

❏ Local-only configuration

Each workstation has Windows and Paradox installed on its local hard disk. Each workstation thus runs Windows and Paradox locally but accesses shared Paradox data in shared network directories.

❏ Combined configuration

Each workstation has Windows installed on its local hard disk but uses a single copy of Paradox with Paradox LAN Licenses on the network. Each workstation thus runs Windows locally but accesses both the Paradox program and shared Paradox data in shared network directories.

❏ Server-only configuration

Each workstation uses a single copy of Windows and a single copy of Paradox with Paradox LAN Licenses on the network. Each workstation thus runs Windows and the Paradox program from the network, and accesses shared Paradox data in shared network directories.

Figure 15-1 shows where Paradox and Windows are installed for each network configuration.

Figure 15-1 Paradox network configurations

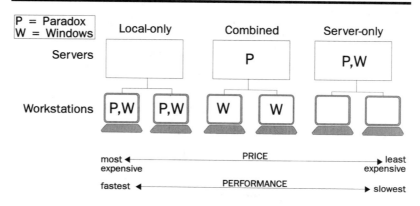

Network concepts

When installing Paradox for network use, you must adhere to the particular license agreement of your Paradox product or products, especially the provisions specifying the number of users authorized to run Paradox concurrently on the network.

Customer Service The Paradox LAN License authorizes one additional user to run Paradox concurrently on a network. Contact Borland Customer Service for complete product information. (See "How to contact Borland" in Chapter 1).

The user count

The user count is the total number of people authorized to run Paradox concurrently on your network. The Paradox title screen displays the current number of users and the total authorized count each time a user starts Paradox. If all the counts available are in use and another user tries to start Paradox, Paradox denies that user access. That user must wait until a current user exits Paradox to make one of the counts available.

You adjust your authorized user count by running the Serial Number Utility. With this utility, you enter the serial number(s) of the Paradox package(s) you've purchased. See "Update the network user count" later in this chapter for information on this program.

Failing to exit properly

If a user working with Paradox on the network fails to exit properly, Paradox doesn't make that user's count available to anyone else. This could occur, for example, when someone is using Paradox and simply turns off the workstation without first ending the Paradox session.

To restore the count, the user needs to log back on to the network from the same workstation; the user doesn't have to restart Paradox. At this point, Paradox detects that the user is no longer working with the program and releases that user's count.

Caution Improperly exiting Paradox, such as by rebooting or shutting off your machine, can cause data loss or corruption.

Network control files

Paradox for Windows uses a network control file called PDOXWIN.USR to keep track of all the Paradox for Windows users on the network. It uses a network control file called PDOXUSRS.NET to control table sharing on the network. DOS Paradox 4.0 uses the PDOXUSRS.NET file to control table sharing *and* to monitor its user count.

PDOXUSRS.NET makes it possible to install and run concurrently both Paradox for Windows and DOS Paradox 4.0 on the network. This allows users of both programs to share data concurrently.

Upgrade all earlier DOS versions of Paradox on the network to DOS Paradox 4.0 or Paradox for Windows.

Versions of DOS Paradox earlier than 4.0 use a PARADOX.NET file to monitor the user count and to control table sharing on the network; thus, neither Paradox for Windows nor DOS Paradox 4.0 users can share data concurrently with users of earlier versions of DOS Paradox. For this reason, you should upgrade earlier versions of DOS Paradox to DOS Paradox 4.0 or to Paradox for Windows.

Table 15-1 The Paradox family of network control files

Network control file	Version(s) used by	Function
PDOXWIN.USR	Paradox for Windows 1.0	Monitor number of Paradox for Windows 1.0 users on the network

Network control file	Version(s) used by	Function
PDOXUSRS.NET	Paradox for Windows 1.0	Control table sharing among Paradox for Windows 1.0 users (and, if applicable, among DOS Paradox 4.0 users)
	DOS Paradox 4.0	Monitor number of DOS Paradox 4.0 users on the network and control table sharing among these users (and, if applicable, among Paradox for Windows 1.0 users)
PARADOX.NET	DOS Paradox versions earlier than 4.0	Monitor number of DOS Paradox 3.5 and earlier version users on the network and control table sharing between these users

Table 15-2 Concurrent table sharing allowed between Paradox products

Version	Paradox for Windows 1.0	DOS Paradox 4.0	DOS Paradox versions earlier than 4.0
Paradox for Windows 1.0	√	√	
DOS Paradox 4.0	√	√	
DOS Paradox versions earlier than 4.0			√

Designating the location of PDOXUSRS.NET

For Paradox for Windows, you designate the location of PDOXUSRS.NET with the ODAPI Configuration Utility. The installation instructions later in this chapter explain how to do this. You must specify a single location, in a shared data directory on the network, to which all Paradox for Windows and, if applicable, DOS Paradox 4.0 users have read/write/create rights. Either Paradox program must be able to find PDOXUSRS.NET in the same place each time a user starts either program.

Note You should not specify a location on a local hard disk for PDOXUSRS.NET; if you do, a user at another workstation might not be able to start Paradox or to access shared data.

The PDOXUSRS.NET file is session-specific. When the first user starts Paradox for Windows or DOS Paradox 4.0 on the network, Paradox for Windows or DOS Paradox 4.0 searches for the file in the location you specified. If either program can't find PDOXUSRS.NET, it creates it in the specified location. Subsequent users will find that the file has already been created. If the file is accidently erased, either program recreates it.

The path name of PDOXUSRS.NET must be the same for each user on the network.

Many network systems allow more than one drive letter to map to a single shared disk drive. Paradox lets you specify different drive letters for the location of PDOXUSRS.NET; however, the path name—everything after the drive letter—must always be the same.

If you don't designate the same PDOXUSRS.NET file location for each user and multiple PDOXUSRS.NET files are active during a Paradox session, some users might be prevented from accessing shared data. People who are using the same PDOXUSRS.NET file can share data, but other users who are using a different PDOXUSRS.NET file can't work with the first group's data.

Dual links

On a network, Paradox identifies tables by their drive letter, path, and table name. Never refer to the same table from one workstation in one session using two different logical drives. Doing so creates a *dual link*, meaning Paradox has two different names *from the same user* for the same table. This could result in serious problems.

Different users at different workstations can access a table with whatever logical drives they choose without problems.

Directories

Before installing and working with Paradox, become familiar with these types of directories:

❒ The ODAPI directory (default: WINDOWS\SYSTEM)

❒ The Paradox system directory (default: PDOXWIN)

❒ Paradox shared data directories (suggested name for the main directory under which these fall: PDOXDATA)

❒ Private directories

❒ Working directories

The ODAPI directory

When you install Paradox, it's set to install the ODAPI files, including ODAPI.CFG, to C:\WINDOWS\SYSTEM by default. These files enable concurrent use of ODAPI programs, including Paradox for Windows and Quattro Pro for Windows.

PATH statement

If the ODAPI files a workstation is using exist somewhere other than WINDOWS\SYSTEM or WINDOWS, that workstation's PATH statement must include the drive and directory containing those ODAPI files.

Rights   All Paradox users must have at least read-only rights to the directory containing the ODAPI files. If a user has just read-only rights to the ODAPI.CFG he or she is using, then that user can't modify that ODAPI.CFG with the ODAPI Configuration Utility.

Local-only configuration

When you install in the local-only configuration, you will probably want to leave the default of C:\WINDOWS\SYSTEM in place, since WINDOWS\SYSTEM is usually located on each local hard disk's drive C in this configuration.

You can install the ODAPI files to a drive and directory other than C:\WINDOWS\SYSTEM; however, if you do, be sure every workstation not using C:\WINDOWS\SYSTEM includes the alternative drive and directory in its PATH statement.

Borland applications use common ODAPI files and look for them at install time in WINDOWS\SYSTEM or WINDOWS. Thus, if you choose to install the ODAPI files to a drive and directory other than C:\WINDOWS\SYSTEM, and you later install another Borland application, you must remember where you installed the original ODAPI files and update them with the more recent ones from the new Borland application.

Combined configuration

In the combined configuration, WINDOWS\SYSTEM usually exists on each workstation's local hard disk drive C. When installing Paradox in this configuration, however, you first install to the network from the network administrator's workstation. Thus, if you leave the default C:\WINDOWS\SYSTEM in place for the ODAPI files, they get installed to the C:\WINDOWS\SYSTEM of the network administrator's workstation. You then have to transfer these files to every other individual workstation's local hard disk.

When first installing Paradox to the network from the network administrator's workstation, install the ODAPI files to a network directory. You can then copy the files from the network to each workstation's local hard disk. The ODAPI files on the network serve as backup files to each workstation's ODAPI files, and the ODAPI.CFG file on the network serves as a default configuration file.

Install the ODAPI files to a separate directory on the network, which you could name ODAPI, for example. After you install, you might want to make the network directory containing the backup and default ODAPI files read-only, in which case users can't then modify the default ODAPI.CFG with the ODAPI Configuration Utility. However, if you have yet to install another ODAPI program, such as

Quattro Pro for Windows, you—as the installer—will need full rights to the ODAPI directory.

Copy the ODAPI files to C:\WINDOWS\SYSTEM on each local hard disk. You can copy the ODAPI files to a drive and directory other than C:\WINDOWS\SYSTEM; however, if you do, be sure every workstation not using C:\WINDOWS\SYSTEM includes the alternative drive and directory in its PATH statement.

Borland applications use common ODAPI files and look for them at install time in WINDOWS\SYSTEM or WINDOWS. Thus, if you choose to copy the ODAPI files to a drive and directory other than C:\WINDOWS\SYSTEM, and you later install another Borland application, you must remember where you installed and copied the original ODAPI files and update them with the more recent ones from the new Borland application.

Following installation in the combined configuration from the network administrator's workstation, you have to set up all workstations. You identify each user's ODAPI.CFG directory with the Local Settings Utility. The installation instructions later in this chapter explain how to do this. See "Using the Local Settings Utility" later in this chapter.

Server-only configuration

When you install in the server-only configuration, install the ODAPI files to the network WINDOWS directory. Edit the default C:\WINDOWS\SYSTEM already in the ODAPI files text box of the INSTALL program. Change the default drive C to the logical network drive you've linked to the WINDOWS directory on the network. Because the network version of Windows installs by default to a WINDOWS directory, not to a WINDOWS\SYSTEM directory, you also need to change the path from WINDOWS\SYSTEM to just WINDOWS.

You can install the ODAPI files to a network directory other than the WINDOWS directory. If you do, however, and these are the ODAPI files you want all of your users to use, each workstation's PATH statement must include the drive and directory containing the ODAPI files.

You can also copy the default ODAPI.CFG to local hard disks to allow users to have individual configurations. In this situation, the ODAPI.CFG on the network serves as a backup and default configuration file. After you install, you might want to make the network directory containing the backup and default ODAPI files read-only, in which case users can't then modify the default ODAPI.CFG with the ODAPI Configuration Utility. However, if you have yet to install another ODAPI program, such as Quattro Pro for Windows, you—as the installer—will need full rights to the ODAPI directory.

If you copy the ODAPI.CFG to local hard disks to allow users to have individual configurations, you'll probably want to copy it to a separate directory—named ODAPI, for example. Be sure to include the drive and directory containing the ODAPI.CFG file the workstation is going to use in the workstation's PATH statement.

Following installation in the server-only configuration from the network administrator's workstation, you have to set up all workstations. You identify each user's ODAPI.CFG directory with the Local Settings Utility. The installation instructions later in this chapter explain how to do this. See "Using the Local Settings Utility" later in this chapter.

The Paradox system directory, PDOXWIN

The Paradox system directory contains the Paradox system, or program, files. Here is a description for each configuration:

❏ When you install Paradox in the local-only configuration, you leave Paradox's default of C:\PDOXWIN in place. You can change drive C to another local hard disk drive, such as D or E. You can also change the default directory name from PDOXWIN to any name you want.

❏ When you install in the combined or server-only configurations, you change the default drive C to the logical network drive on the network where you want to install Paradox. We also recommend you make it a subdirectory of a network shared applications directory, if you have one. You can change the default directory name from PDOXWIN to any name you want.

Make PDOXWIN on the network read-only after installation.

Following installation in the combined or server-only configurations, you might want to make the directory where you installed the system files read-only, or make the Paradox system files read-only. Some networks don't allow multiple users to execute programs concurrently if the program's files aren't read-only.

Shared data directory, PDOXDATA

For all three network configurations, create at least one shared data directory on the network to which all Paradox users have read/write/create rights. You need one such directory for the PDOXUSRS.NET control file, and you need one to store shared Paradox objects. One shared directory can serve both purposes. Name this directory PDOXDATA.

Give all network Paradox users full rights to PDOXDATA.

All users must have read/write/create rights to the network directory containing PDOXUSRS.NET, because the first user to start Paradox creates this file, and all users read from and write to that file during their Paradox sessions.

Private directories

Paradox uses private directories to store each user's temporary Paradox objects, such as *Answer* tables. Temporary objects created by each user must be stored in a unique directory; otherwise, one user's temporary objects would overwrite another's. Every person who uses Paradox on the network must have a private directory when running Paradox.

When you install in the local-only configuration, Paradox automatically creates a subdirectory it names PRIVATE under the PDOXWIN system directory. PDOXWIN\PRIVATE is the default private directory in the local-only configuration.

In the combined and server-only configurations, Paradox detects that you're installing to a network rather than a local drive and thus doesn't automatically create a PRIVATE subdirectory under PDOXWIN on the network. In these configurations, if you don't specify a private directory for a user, Paradox uses the Windows temporary directory as that user's private directory. This will work in the combined configuration, where each workstation has a local WINDOWS\TEMP. In the server-only configuration, where Windows and its single temporary directory exist on the network, you must specify a separate unique directory as the private directory for each workstation.

Consider making the following directories the private directory for the following network environments:

❑   If a workstation has a local hard disk, use C:\PDOXWIN in the combined and server-only configurations and C:\PDOXWIN\PRIVATE in the local-only configuration.

❑   If a workstation has no local hard disk, make the workstation user's network home directory the private directory. The user must have read/write/create rights to the directory.

Keep these things in mind when specifying private directories:

❑   You can't use a floppy disk drive as a private directory.

❑   If a user performs queries on large tables, the private directory should be located on a drive with adequate disk space.

You identify each user's private directory with the Local Settings Utility. The installation instructions later in this chapter explain how to do this. See "Using the Local Settings Utility" later in this chapter for information on this program.

You can override the default location of the private directory that the Local Settings Utility specifies with the command-line option **-p**. See "Overriding directories" later in this chapter for instructions.

Working directories

Two working directories are in effect when you run Paradox:

❐ The Program Item Properties dialog box contains a Command Line text box and Working Directory text box. If you don't put the drive and full path to the PDOXWIN.EXE in the Command Line text box, then you must put this information in the Working Directory text box. See Figures 15-7 and 15-8 later in this chapter for examples of your two choices.

❐ The Paradox data working directory contains the Paradox data files you're working with. When you install in the local-only configuration, Paradox automatically creates a subdirectory it names WORKING under the PDOXWIN system directory. PDOXWIN\WORKING is the default working directory in the local-only configuration.

In the combined and server-only configurations, Paradox detects that you're installing to a network rather than a local drive and thus doesn't automatically create a WORKING subdirectory under PDOXWIN on the network. Specify each workstation's working directory with the Local Settings Utility. The installation instructions later in this chapter explain how to do this. See "Using the Local Settings Utility" later in this chapter for information on this program.

You can override the default location of the Paradox data files working directory that the Local Settings Utility specifies with the command-line option **-w**. See "Overriding directories" later in this chapter for instructions.

Note

If the Paradox data working directory is a network shared directory, multiple users can access its data concurrently. If a user designates a network directory as a private directory, this prevents all other users from working with objects stored there. Paradox informs other users of the name of the user who's made the directory private when they try to access its data.

Figure 15-2 Location of directories in the local-only configuration

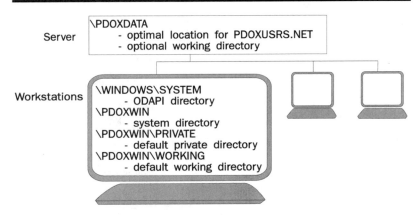

Figure 15-3 Location of directories in the combined configuration

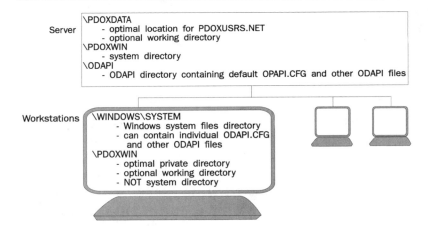

Figure 15-4 Location of directories in the server-only configuration

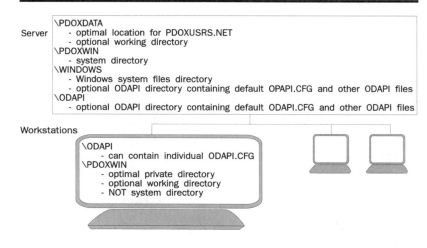

Server

```
\PDOXDATA
    - optimal location for PDOXUSRS.NET
    - optional working directory
\PDOXWIN
    - system directory
\WINDOWS
    - Windows system files directory
    - optional ODAPI directory containing default OPAPI.CFG and other ODAPI files
\ODAPI
    - optional ODAPI directory containing default ODAPI.CFG and other ODAPI files
```

Workstations

```
\ODAPI
    - can contain individual ODAPI.CFG
\PDOXWIN
    - optimal private directory
    - optional working directory
    - NOT system directory
```

Installing Paradox

With each of the three Paradox network configurations, you must first install Windows and then Paradox at one workstation. This section assumes the one workstation you start with is the network administrator's workstation.

Install Windows

Follow the Windows installation instructions in the Windows printed and online documentation:

❏ For the local-only and combined configurations, install an individual, standalone copy of Windows on the local hard disk of each workstation.

❏ For the server-only configuration, install the network version of Windows on the network, using the network administrator's workstation. After installing Windows on the network, set up each workstation to access Windows, following Windows printed and online documentation.

Install Paradox

After Windows is installed, install Paradox:

❏ For the local-only configuration, install an individual, standalone copy of Paradox on the local hard disk of each workstation, following the instructions in Chapter 2 of this manual.

❏ For the combined and server-only configurations, install on the network an individual, standalone copy of Paradox, using the network administrator's workstation. After installing Paradox on the network, set up each workstation to access it; follow the instructions in the next section.

Combined and server-only configurations

After installing Paradox on the network in the combined or server-only configurations, link all other workstations to the program. If you're installing in the local-only configuration, skip this section and proceed with "Run the Local Settings Utility."

Update the network user count

From the network administrator's workstation, use the Serial Number Utility to update the user count on the network by entering the serial numbers of additional Paradox packages you've purchased. With the Serial Number Utility, you can also change the user and company names.

Caution   Use the Serial Number Utility to modify Paradox network installation parameters only when no Paradox users are on the network.

To modify network installation parameters with the Serial Number Utility,

1. Before you start the program, make sure no one is using Paradox on the network.

2. In the Paradox program group window, double-click the Serial Number Utility icon. The Serial Number Update Program dialog box appears with your current serial numbers, user name, and company name.

Figure 15-5 Serial Number Update Program dialog box

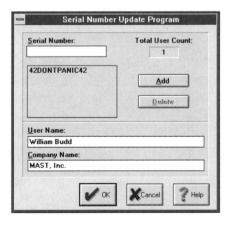

3. Add or delete serial numbers to adjust your user count:

❑ To add serial numbers, type the new serial numbers, one at a time, in the Serial Number text box and choose Add. Each new serial number appears in the box below the Serial Number text box each time you choose Add.

If you try to add an invalid serial number, you get an error message when you choose Add. If the serial number you've entered matches the one on one of your program disks, make sure they're Paradox program disks and that it's a Paradox serial number. If they are Paradox program disks, call Borland Technical Support. (See Chapter 1 of this manual for instructions for calling Borland Technical Support.)

❑ To delete serial numbers, select numbers, one at a time, in the box below the Serial Number text box and choose Delete. The serial number you selected disappears from this box when you choose Delete.

4. When you're finished adding and/or deleting serial numbers, choose OK.

Create Paradox program groups at each workstation (optional)

At each workstation, you can create a program group window for Paradox in Windows. (The network administrator's workstation already has the Paradox program group window, because the installation program created it automatically.) If you want Paradox in another existing program group window, skip this section and proceed with "Create Paradox icons at each workstation."

At each workstation, start Windows and

1. Choose File | New from the Windows Program Manager menu.

2. In the New Program Object dialog box, choose Program Group, then choose OK.

3. Type a description for the Paradox program group in the Description text box, such as **Paradox for Windows**.

4. Choose OK. An empty Paradox program group window appears with the description you typed as its title.

Figure 15-6 Paradox for Windows program group window

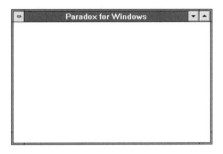

Create Paradox icons at each workstation

At each workstation, create the Paradox icon in the Paradox program group window. (The network administrator's workstation already has the Paradox icon in the Paradox program group window, because the installation program created it automatically.)

1. With the Paradox program group window selected, choose File | New from the Windows Program Manager menu.

2. In the New Program Object dialog box, choose Program Item and choose OK.

3. Type a description for Paradox in the Description text box, such as **Paradox for Windows**.

4. Specify the drive and full path to PDOXWIN.EXE on the network in one of the following ways:

   ❑ In the Command Line text box, type the drive and full path to PDOXWIN.EXE on the network, followed by the file name PDOXWIN.EXE.

Figure 15-7 Drive\path in Command Line text box

   ❑ Type the file name PDOXWIN.EXE in the Command Line text box, and type the drive and full path to PDOXWIN.EXE's directory in the Working Directory text box, in which case you must include this drive and directory (default: PDOXWIN) in the path statement.

Figure 15-8 Drive\path in Working Directory text box

Note

The working directory you're defining in the Program Item Properties dialog box is distinct from the Paradox data working directory, which you define with Paradox's Local Settings Utility. See "Working directories" under "Directories" earlier in this chapter for details.

5. Choose OK. A Network Path Specified dialog box appears, warning you that this program is located on a network directory and thus might not always be available.

Figure 15-9 Network Path Specified dialog box

6. Choose Yes. The Paradox icon appears in the Paradox program group window.

Figure 15-10 Paradox icon in the program group window

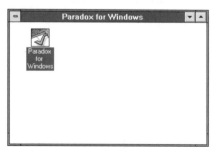

Create Paradox utility icons at each workstation

At each workstation, create the ODAPI Configuration Utility, Table Utility, and Local Settings Utility icons in the Paradox program group window. (You can also create the Serial Number Utility icon at each workstation, but since this utility is for updating the user count, you might want to keep it only on the network administrator's workstation.) Follow the same instructions in the previous section for each utility, substituting the values in Table 15-3 for the Description and .EXE file parameters.

Table 15-3 Utility descriptions and .EXE files

Utility	Description	.EXE file
ODAPI Configuration	ODAPI Configuration Utility	ODAPICFG.EXE
Table Repair	Table Repair Utility	TUTILITY.EXE
Local Settings	Local Settings Utility	PWLOCAL.EXE
Serial Number	Serial Number Utility	PWUPDATE.EXE

All of these utility .EXE files are in the system directory (PDOXWIN) with PDOXWIN.EXE. When you're finished creating the utility icons, the Paradox group window should look like Figure 15-11.

Figure 15-11 Paradox for Windows icons

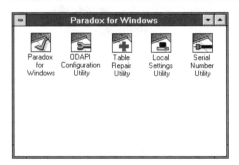

Run the Local Settings Utility

Specify the location of each user's private and working directories and the ODAPI configuration file, ODAPI.CFG, with the Local Settings Utility. At each workstation,

1. Run the Local Settings Utility. Double-click the Local Settings Utility icon in the Paradox program group window. In any of the configurations, you might encounter an Error dialog box. This dialog box informs you that you're missing or need to update the BWCC.DLL file.

Figure 15-12 The Error dialog box

BWCC is an acronym for Borland Windows Custom Control. You must have this file in the WINDOWS\SYSTEM or WINDOWS directory the workstation is using to run Paradox. Click OK to copy the up-to-date BWCC.DLL (that came with the other Paradox program files) from the PDOXWIN directory to the WINDOWS\SYSTEM or WINDOWS directory the workstation is using. The Paradox for Windows Local Settings dialog box appears.

Figure 15-13 Paradox for Windows Local Settings dialog box

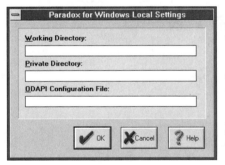

In the combined and server-only configurations, all text boxes will be empty at all workstations except the network administrator's

In the local-only configuration, the Working Directory text box will contain C:\PDOXWIN\WORKING, the Private Directory text box will contain C:\PDOXWIN\PRIVATE, and the ODAPI Configuration File text box will contain the drive and path to the ODAPI.CFG file and the file name ODAPI.CFG

2. In the Working Directory text box, type the drive and full path to the local or network directory you want to be your default Paradox data files working directory. The data files working directory is not the same as the DOS working directory, which should be the system directory (PDOXWIN). See "Working directories" earlier in this chapter for an explanation of the difference.

   ☐ In the local-only configuration, the Working Directory text box should already contain the drive and full path to the subdirectory WORKING under the directory where you installed Paradox on the local hard disk. If you installed to the default drive and directory, the Working Directory text box contains C:\PDOXWIN\WORKING.

   You can leave the C:\PDOXWIN\WORKING default in place, or you can change it. For example, you might want to set a

beginning Paradox for Windows user's working directory to
C:\PDOXWIN\SAMPLE, where the sample files are located
(assuming you installed them and put them in SAMPLE). Or,
you might want to set some user's working directory to a
network shared data directory, such as PDOXDATA.

❏ In the combined and server-only configurations, at every
workstation except the network administrator's workstation,
the Working Directory text box will be empty. You need to
specify a working directory for each workstation.

As with the local-only configuration, specify a working
directory that suits that workstation's user's needs. If a user is
a Paradox for Windows beginner, you might want to set his or
her working directory to the directory containing the sample
files. If a user works mostly with shared data on the network,
set his or her working directory to a network shared data
directory, such as PDOXDATA.

Tip   When using a local-only or combined configuration, it's best to
create a network directory (PDOXDATA) for users who share
tables and other files. You can also use this directory as the
location of the PDOXUSRS.NET file.

See also   For more information, see "Configure Paradox for sharing data on
a network" later in this chapter.

3. In the Private Directory text box, type the drive and full path to
the local or network directory you want to be the default private
directory for that workstation. Each Paradox network user must
have a unique private directory in which to store temporary
objects, such as *Answer* tables. No two users can have the same
private directory.

❏ In the local-only configuration, the Private Directory text box
should already contain the drive and full path to the
subdirectory PRIVATE under the directory where you installed
Paradox on the local hard disk. If you installed to the default
drive and directory, the Private Directory text box contains
C:\PDOXWIN\PRIVATE. You can leave the C:\PDOXWIN\
PRIVATE default in place, since this directory is on the local
hard drive.

❏ In the combined and server-only configurations, at every
workstation except the network administrator's, the Private
Directory text box will be empty.

If the workstation has a local hard disk, create a PDOXWIN
directory on the local hard disk and make C:\PDOXWIN the
private directory.

If the workstation doesn't have a local hard disk, make the private directory the workstation user's home directory on the network. The user must have full rights to this directory.

4. In the ODAPI Configuration File text box, type the drive and full path to ODAPI.CFG and the file name ODAPI.CFG.

❏ In the local-only configuration, the ODAPI Configuration File text box should already contain the drive and full path to the directory where you installed the ODAPI files on the local hard disk. If you installed to the default drive and directory, the ODAPI Configuration File text box contains C:\WINDOWS\SYSTEM\ODAPI.CFG.

You can leave the C:\WINDOWS\SYSTEM\ODAPI.CFG default in place. If you change the drive or path to ODAPI.CFG, you must relocate ODAPI.CFG accordingly.

See "Local-only configuration" under "The ODAPI directory" earlier in this chapter for a full discussion of why you might want to use a directory other than WINDOWS\SYSTEM for the ODAPI files.

❏ In the combined and server-only configurations, at every workstation except the network administrator's, the ODAPI Configuration File text box will be empty.

Type the drive and full path to the default ODAPI.CFG file on the network, if that's the only ODAPI.CFG file you want the users to use. If you copy the ODAPI.CFG file to the workstation's local hard disk—to allow each user to modify the default configuration to an individual configuration—type the drive and full path to the local ODAPI.CFG file and the file name ODAPI.CFG. Be sure to include the local drive and path to the local ODAPI.CFG in the workstation's path statement.

See "Combined configuration" and "Server-only configuration" under "The ODAPI directory" earlier in this chapter for a full discussion of why you might want to locate the ODAPI files in various directories, both on the network and locally.

Configure Paradox for sharing data on a network

After you've installed Paradox, you need to configure each workstation to access data on a network. This involves running the ODAPI Configuration Utility to specify the location of PDOXUSRS.NET.

You must specify the same network directory location of PDOXUSRS.NET for each workstation. Do *not* specify a local hard disk directory for the location of PDOXUSRS.NET. At each workstation,

1. Run the ODAPI Configuration Utility. Double-click the Configuration Utility icon in the Paradox program group window. The ODAPI Configuration Utility dialog box appears.

Figure 15-14 ODAPI Configuration Utility dialog box

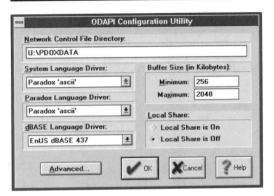

2. In the Network Control File Directory text box, type the drive and full path to PDOXUSRS.NET on the network. Store PDOXUSRS.NET in the main Paradox shared data directory (PDOXDATA). This step assumes you've already created this directory on the network and given every user read/write/create access to it.

Run Paradox at each workstation

In all configurations, after you've installed Paradox at each workstation and configured it to access shared data on the network, run the program at each workstation. If Paradox doesn't start at any one of the workstations, review the sections prior to this one and redo them, if necessary.

Overriding directories

Each user can override the default private and working directory locations specified in the Local Settings Utility with the command-line options **-p** and **-w**, respectively.

Overriding the default private directory

To override the default private directory specified in the Local Settings Utility with the command-line option **-p**,

1. Highlight the Paradox icon and choose File | Properties from the Windows Program Manager menu.

2. Choose OK while Program Item is selected. The Progam Item Properties dialog box appears.

3. In the Command Line text box of the Program Item Properties dialog box, type a space after the drive and path name of PDOXWIN.EXE and then type

   -p C:\NEWDIR

   where NEWDIR is the new private directory. You can also change the drive. A user with a diskless workstation can't specify the hard disk drive C but must instead specify a network drive, just as in the Local Settings Utility.

   The private directory must always be unique to the user; it can't be shared by more than one user. Users should be careful when specifying private directories not to specify a shared working data directory. If they do, they'll prevent all other users from accessing that data.

Overriding the default working directory

To override the default working directory specified in the Local Settings Utility with the command-line option **-w**, either before or after the **-p** parameters (or by itself after the drive and path to PDOXWIN.EXE, if you're only specifying a new working directory), type a space and then type

-w C:\NEWDIR

where NEWDIR is the new Paradox data files working directory. You can also change the drive. A user with a diskless workstation can't specify the hard disk drive C but must instead specify a network drive, just as in the Local Settings Utility.

Note The working directory you specify with the Local Settings Utility or with the command-line option **-w** is not the same as the DOS working directory you can specify in the Working Directory text box of the Windows 3.1 Program Item Properties dialog box. See "Working directories" under "Directories" earlier in this chapter for details.

CHAPTER 16

International issues

Paradox fully supports character sets, data formats, and sorting conventions commonly used outside the United States. This chapter provides an overview of Paradox's international features and describes how it handles different

- ❐ Character sets

- ❐ Sorting conventions

- ❐ Data formats

Note   These issues are of particular interest to those working in international environments, but they apply to all users.

Preparation and assumptions

Before installing Paradox in (or using tables from) an international setting, make sure of the following:

- ❐ The appropriate code page and country drivers are installed in CONFIG.SYS.

- ❐ The International settings of Windows Control Panel correspond to your needs.

- ❐ You understand the differences between (and implications of) the Windows (ANSI) character set and your DOS (OEM) code page.

- ❐ You know how to use *Alt* and the numeric keypad to enter extended characters in Windows applications and files. (Make sure NumLock is on before attempting this.)

See also   For more information about these issues and concepts, consult your Windows and DOS documentation.

Character set issues

Because Paradox is a Windows application, it supports the ANSI
character set for files that can be used only by other Windows
applications. This includes forms, reports, scripts, and libraries.
However, because tables can be used by non-Windows applications
(for example, Paradox 4.0), Paradox stores OEM characters in tables.
This means Paradox translates ANSI characters to those in your OEM
code page when saving table data.

For example, if you're using code page 437 (the default code page for
U.S. workstations) and place an "Æ" (ANSI character 198) in a field,
Paradox saves it as OEM character 146. You'll see the same character
when viewing the table, but it's not literally the same one you
originally entered.

Most of the time, this is transparent; that is, there is no loss of data.
However, if you enter a character that is *not* supported by your code
page, Paradox converts it to one that is. For example, if you're using
code page 437 and type an "Õ", Paradox converts it to an "O"
because your code page doesn't support the original character. In this
example, a mild form of data loss occurs; the tilde (~) is removed.

If you enter an ANSI character that can't be converted to a similar
character in your code page, Paradox replaces it with OEM character
254 (□).

Character conversion occurs when you

❑ Enter data into a table

❑ Name a file

❑ Export data to OEM files or applications

In all other operations, Paradox uses and saves characters from the
ANSI character set.

Preventing character conversion

If you want to prevent Paradox from converting characters, use the
Strict Translation command from the Table or Form menu while
editing a table. If you turn Strict Translation on and try to save a
record containing characters that are not supported by your code
page, Paradox displays the message **Character(s) not supported by
Table Language** and prevents you from saving the record until you

❑ Remove (or replace) the unsupported characters

❑ Turn Strict Translation off

Sorting conventions

Paradox uses *language drivers* to sort tables according to different conventions. If you're using a workstation with non-U.S. settings or are working with tables created on non-U.S. workstations, make sure Paradox is using the language driver(s) closest to the conventions you're used to.

In most cases, you should not have to worry about a table's language drivers after setting the default drivers for your workstation. When sharing tables between workstations, make sure the workstations are using the same default language drivers.

Changing the default language drivers

To change Paradox's default language drivers, run the Configuration Utility, click the drop-down arrow next to the driver you want to change, and then choose the driver you want from the list that appears. Each language driver is appropriate only for a particular code page; for example, the Paradox International (Paradox 'intl') driver works with code page 437 only. Use language drivers appropriate for your code page. To see the language drivers appropriate for each code page, see the online Help system of the Configuration Utility.

Changing language drivers for Paradox tables

When working with Paradox tables, you can assign different language drivers to different tables. To change a table's language driver,

1. Restructure it (by choosing File | Utilities | Restructure or Table | Restructure).

2. Choose Table Language from the Table Properties panel.

3. Choose Modify, then choose the driver you want.

4. Choose OK to save your changes.

Use the Configuration Utility to change the default language driver for your Paradox tables.

Changing language drivers for dBASE tables

When working with dBASE tables, Paradox uses the default dBASE language driver you chose in the Configuration Utility. If you change this driver, all dBASE tables will be sorted according to the rules of the new driver.

These rules also affect the structure of your tables. For example, with the dBASE German language driver (De dBASE 437), you can name a field "FÖÖ." You can't do this using the dBASE English U.S. driver (EnUS dBASE 437).

See also For more information about changing default language drivers, see Chapter 14.

Working with tables using different language drivers

Although you can use different language drivers for different Paradox tables, we advise against linking tables using different language drivers. This includes (but is not limited to) operations like the following:

❐ Joining tables using different language drivers in queries

❐ Adding or subtracting two tables based on different language drivers

❐ Creating multi-table documents based on tables with different language drivers

❐ Defining referential integrity between tables based on different language drivers

❐ Defining a lookup table using a table based on a language driver different than the master table.

Paradox is designed to handle such operations; however some language driver combinations may yield unexpected results. For best results, choose one language driver, then restructure your tables so they use that driver.

Note You can use Paradox language drivers only for Paradox tables and dBASE language drivers for dBASE tables.

Data formats

In Paradox, the default symbols and formats used for your data are based on the International settings in the Windows Control Panel. For example, if you set your Windows Control Panel currency symbol to "£", Paradox uses it when displaying currency values. Similarly, Paradox formats date and time values according to the settings used by Windows.

To set Paradox's defaults *permanently* to different formats, begin by changing the appropriate International settings in the Windows Control Panel. When you change an International setting in the Windows Control Panel, it affects the default formats used in all Paradox operations, *except* some internal data conversion operations.

Internal data conversion

Many operations require Paradox to convert a string of characters to a number, date, or time value. For example, when you enter a date into a table, Paradox converts the characters you type to a value representing a date. This process is automatic and generally uses format settings in Windows Control Panel to control the conversion. However, a few operations use ODAPI to convert character strings to number, date, or time values and to convert these data formats to character strings. These operations include

❐ Queries that use selection criteria or perform pattern matching on number and date fields

❐ Table restructures that change alphanumeric fields to number or date fields (and the reverse)

❐ Adding or subtracting records between tables that do *not* have the same structure

Because these operations use ODAPI for this internal data conversion, you *must* ensure ODAPI.CFG uses the same data format conventions and settings as Windows Control Panel; otherwise, unexpected results might occur.

Note This doesn't affect the way data is formatted when you display it; Paradox uses the settings in Windows Control Panel to display data.

We recommend using standard data formats when possible. In most cases, you won't have to worry about these settings, because ODAPI (when installed) is configured to the data format conventions of the country defined in Windows Control Panel. However, if you customize Windows Control Panel so it uses settings that are different from your country's data format conventions, you should also configure ODAPI to the same settings; otherwise, queries that match date and numeric values may yield unexpected results.

For example, the "forward-slash" (/) is commonly used in U.S. workstations as a date separator. If you change this to an ampersand (&) in Windows Control Panel, you should also configure ODAPI so it uses an ampersand for a date separator.

Caution We *strongly* recommend making a backup of ODAPI.CFG before changing it with the Configuration Utility.

To configure ODAPI to specialized date, time, or number formats,

1. Start the Configuration Utility.

2. Choose the Advanced button.

3. Choose System | Formats.

4. Choose the format type you changed in Windows Control Panel.

5. Choose a setting you changed in Windows Control Panel.

6. Enter the new value in the Value text box.

7. Repeat steps 4 through 7 as needed.

8. Choose OK twice to save your changes.

You can also update ODAPI to the current settings in Windows Control Panel by reinstalling ODAPI. For more information, see Chapter 2.

See also For more information and a description of the settings in ODAPI, see the online help system of the Configuration Utility.

Note If you customize ODAPI so it uses special number formats, you may not be able to share saved queries with other workstations unless those workstations have also been customized to the same settings.

Tip If you want a special format for a specific table or field, change the appropriate Format properties. For more information, see Chapter 4 in the *User's Guide*.

X

Z